"An excellent read—full of guidance and practical, ageless wisdom for teens who are looking to better themselves."

—**Robert W. Hasselmann, MA**, middle school teacher, Robbins, IL

"As with other books written by the author on this subject, this is easy to read, makes sense, and easy to apply with my clients individually, in group settings, or in family therapy sessions. My clients' ages range between ten and twenty-three, and many are at-risk youth, children, and families. I like using the book for ideas to assist clients who struggle with depression, bullying, and anxiety. They find the information applicable as they read and journal, and we process new skills. The information is therapeutic and backed by empirically sound research. This is not merely a 'self-help' book. This book is a great tool I've added to my counseling toolbox."

—**Nancy DeWeese, MAMHC, LPC**, family therapist with Professional Services Group

"Excellent resource that can be used by everyone—young and old! 'Perceive it, believe it, achieve it!' is a thought and activity process in the book that can be used in every area of life. In addition, the fifty simple ways to build confidence are just that—simple. Finally, the exercises are easily personalized for each person. Highly recommended! Great workbook!"

—**Kim Kanish**, blended case manager, Family Psychological Association

"Lisa Schab's *The Self-Esteem Habit for Teens* is a well-articulated definition of self-esteem and how a teen can acquire and strengthen it in their life. It's really simple and easy to follow, builds on itself, and it's *not* boring.... This manual is a 'must-have' for any teen who wants to feel good about themselves."

—**Edward J. Nekarda, LCSW, BCD, MDiv**,
    psychotherapist in private practice, attention deficit/
    hyperactivity disorder (ADHD) specialist, and
    certified rapid trauma resolution therapist

"A wonderful resource and guide for all ages. The exercises in this book are easy to follow and there is something to appeal to almost everyone looking for a self-esteem boost or reset. I finished reading with the thought that I wish I would have had this when I was a teen."

—**Ann Almgren**, president at Harvard Diggins City
    Library Board, Harvard Diggins Library, Harvard, IL

the *instant* help solutions series

Young people today need mental health resources more than ever. That's why New Harbinger created the **Instant Help Solutions Series** especially for teens. Written by leading psychologists, physicians, and professionals, these evidence-based self-help books offer practical tips and strategies for dealing with a variety of mental health issues and life challenges teens face, such as depression, anxiety, bullying, eating disorders, trauma, and self-esteem problems.

Studies have shown that young people who learn healthy coping skills early on are better able to navigate problems later in life. Engaging and easy-to-use, these books provide teens with the tools they need to thrive—at home, at school, and on into adulthood.

This series is part of the **New Harbinger Instant Help Books** imprint, founded by renowned child psychologist Lawrence Shapiro. For a complete list of books in this series, visit newharbinger.com.

THE SELF-ESTEEM HABIT FOR TEENS

50 simple ways to build your confidence every day

LISA M. SCHAB, LCSW

Instant Help Books
An Imprint of New Harbinger Publications, Inc.

Publisher's Note

This publication is designed to provide accurate and authoritative information in regard to the subject matter covered. It is sold with the understanding that the publisher is not engaged in rendering psychological, financial, legal, or other professional services. If expert assistance or counseling is needed, the services of a competent professional should be sought.

Distributed in Canada by Raincoast Books

Copyright © 2017 by Lisa M. Schab

                Instant Help Books
                An imprint of New Harbinger Publications, Inc.
                5674 Shattuck Avenue
                Oakland, CA 94609
                www.newharbinger.com

Cover design by Amy Shoup

Acquired by Tesilya Hanauer

Edited by Karen Schader

All Rights Reserved

Library of Congress Cataloging-in-Publication Data on file

19   18   17

10 9 8 7 6 5 4 3 2 1   First Printing

This book is dedicated to my great-grandfather
Louis A. Wiemann (1854–1934), a wise and
successful man—with healthy self-esteem!

My Philosophies of Life

by Louis Wiemann

Be good. The straight path is the only path that leads to Health and Happiness.

Do the best you can with your own faults—as nobody is perfect.

Associate with happy people.

Look at Life from the right angle and remember that on the whole your disappointments most likely were beneficial.

Have a Plan in Life and a Hobby.

Use one thing to balance another.

If you are a mental worker choose a Hobby which requires exercise and vice versa…

Change your surrounding sometimes.

If you don't travel, alter the interior of your house, office, et cetera…

Belong to some club.

Belong to some religion.

Believe in people. Don't allow any of your disappointments to destroy your faith in people.

Contents

get started: the first six steps to healthy self-esteem

Welcome to this book! If you're here because you want to feel good about yourself, you're in the right place. This book will teach you the thoughts and actions that build healthy self-esteem. You can actually make a habit of feeling good about yourself. The only requirements are desire and practice. If you want healthy self-esteem and you continually practice making the choices that produce it, you can achieve it.

The six steps described in this chapter will give you the foundation you need for reaching your goal. The steps are progressive, so it's most helpful to learn them in order. Understanding step 1 will give you information you need to use step 2. When you've learned step 2, you're better able to practice step 3, and so on. These six steps give you a base of information to fall back on as you practice choosing new behaviors. They're the first part of your path to healthy self-esteem.

The rest of the book takes you further down the path, teaching the thoughts and actions that build healthy self-esteem. You can use these tools just about any time, anywhere, and in any situation; all you need is yourself and the decision to try. The more often you use them, the more effective they'll be.

Whether you're starting out on pretty good terms with yourself or you've never had healthy self-esteem before, take a minute now to consciously open your mind to the possibility; plant the seeds for a deep knowing that this can happen for you. Create a new space within yourself where your healthy self-esteem is going to grow. Then, take the first step...

Step 1. Understand your goal: healthy self-esteem.

To work toward something effectively you have to be clear about what you're striving for. This book is about creating healthy self-esteem, so it's important to understand what that means. Some people say they have healthy self-esteem but really feel good about themselves only by thinking they're superior to others. Some people say they have healthy self-esteem but really feel good only about who they're pretending to be, not their real selves.

Healthy self-esteem comes from knowing and accepting your real self at the deepest level, with all your strengths and flaws. It comes from truly understanding your equality to others and their equality to you. It comes from acting on that truth by approaching your own vulnerability and that of others with compassion, and being strong enough inside to stand up for your beliefs while at the same time tolerating differences and respecting the rights of others.

When you have healthy self-esteem, you are confident enough to act with integrity and self-discipline and take responsibility for your thoughts, feelings, and actions. You use healthy coping skills to meet life's challenges. When you make mistakes, you accept them and get back in the game. When someone rejects you, you let yourself grieve, and then let go and move on. When you have successes, you celebrate them fully, but you don't think or act like you're better than anyone else.

People with healthy self-esteem might say things like:

"I can see my part in this problem."

"I have some weaknesses but I'm working on them."

"I wonder if they'll like me."

"I have a really different opinion from theirs."

"I'm having a hard time learning this but I'm going to keep trying."

In the same circumstances people with unhealthy self-esteem might say things like:

"It's all your fault we've got this problem."

"I don't have any weaknesses."

"I'm sure they won't like me."

"People with that opinion are idiots."

"I'm having a hard time learning this; I can't do anything right."

Healthy self-esteem is an anchor that keeps you grounded and steady as you move through life. It helps you bring courage, confidence, and kindness to every situation and every person you encounter—including yourself. When you have healthy self-esteem, you have a better chance for happiness and success in everything you do.

Step 2. Know that your self-esteem is in your hands.

You might think your self-esteem is a product of your upbringing, your environment, or your life circumstances. You might think things like "I can't have healthy self-esteem because my parents always put me down," or "…I live in a bad neighborhood," or "…I'm slow at reading," or "…I don't like my eyes."

Everyone can find some reason not to have healthy self-esteem; we all have challenges to overcome. But the truth is, self-esteem isn't dependent on anything outside yourself. No matter what your childhood or your life or your skills or your body looks like, your self-esteem doesn't come from those outer factors. Self-esteem comes from what you think about yourself. And what you think about yourself is *your* choice.

For example, you might hear someone say, "You'll never amount to anything; you're too lazy," and believe him. You might think, "He's right. I just don't have what it takes." And because you choose that thought you'll feel bad about yourself. However, you could hear the same words and *not* believe them. You could think, "He doesn't realize what I'm capable of; I have drive and energy and talent, and I'm going to do great things!" And because you choose that thought you'll feel good about yourself. You can struggle in school—or sports or friendships or family—and think, "I'm such a loser because math is hard for me," or "I didn't make the team," or "My friend betrayed me," or "My family's messed up." Or you can think, "These are challenges I have to face, but they don't make me a loser. They're outer circumstances. They don't affect my worth."

Your self-esteem is a product of your own thoughts. These thoughts may be influenced by what others tell you, what you experience, and the tendency for your brain to think negatively or positively. But ultimately, you can decide which thoughts you hold on to, which you let go of, and which you believe. You can dislike your eyes and think, "My eyes aren't considered as attractive as some people's, so I'm not as good as them." Or you can think, "My eyes have absolutely nothing to do with my worth. I have the same value as everyone else on the planet."

Your self-esteem comes from the thoughts you choose to believe about yourself. Most of us need some practice with this, and that's the purpose of this book—to help you learn what and how to practice.

Step 3. **Believe in your intrinsic value and worth.**

Some people believe they make mistakes or get into trouble because they're just bad at the core of their being. Some people believe if they've been abandoned or abused it's because there's something inherently wrong with them. Some people believe that no matter what they do or say they're just no good. It's important to know that none of these beliefs is true. What is true is that no matter who you are or where you come from, *you have value simply because you exist*. It doesn't matter how many times you've messed up, fallen short, or been rejected, or how many things you don't like about yourself. None of those things changes the fact that you—like everyone else—came into this world with essential value and worth. Nothing you do or say can change that.

Imagine the nursery in a hospital maternity ward with dozens of tiny newborns sleeping and gurgling in their soft beds. Look more closely: is there a divider splitting the room to make one section for babies who have value and the other for those who don't? Of course not. Because every single life that arrives on earth comes in with the same importance, the same significance, the same value. The room is filled with new lives that are all natural wonders and all miracles.

Humans are pretty amazing. Our bodies, minds, and spirits are remarkable systems of waves, particles, and energy patterns working in sync to sustain us—far beyond the ability of any computer microchip. Our personalities, intellect, emotions, and potential are unique to our species. The fact that you are reading this book right now—eyes, brain, heart, lungs all running in unison without even being programmed—is incredible. Each of us is a spectacular creation.

When you understand that we're all the same in this way, you can grasp everyone's innate and equal value. We might look, think, talk, or act differently, but underneath it all everyone is made of the same stuff; we all showed up as valuable sparks of life. This fact is a cornerstone for healthy self-esteem. Even if you've gotten messages otherwise or have negative thoughts about yourself, no matter what happened between the day you were born and today your value did not change. No matter what you do or say, or how long you live, your intrinsic value is always there. Your understanding of this truth opens the door to self-acceptance. It gives you the foundation you need to choose thoughts and actions that create healthy self-esteem.

Step 4. **Be your authentic self.**

At one time or another most of us have thought we might feel better about ourselves if we were someone else. We've thought we'd be happier with another person's life, personality, circumstances, looks, brain, or skills. We've thought if we could only be more like that person we could finally like ourselves; we could finally have healthy self-esteem.

But as we've already shown, self-esteem comes from our thoughts. It doesn't come from personality, life circumstances, looks, intelligence, or talents. In fact, it's possible that even if we were someone else, we still wouldn't choose the thoughts that create healthy self-esteem. It's even possible that the very person we're trying to be like doesn't have healthy self-esteem either. It all depends on how that person thinks of himself or herself, not what we see from the outside.

People are all different for a reason; diversity is essential to our species. You aren't meant to be someone else, you're meant to be you. Your *authentic self*—the person you truly are deep down inside—holds the clues to the path that's right for you and the gifts that you'll contribute to the planet. If you're perfectly orchestrated to contribute through your speaking, coding, skating, or gardening skills, then that's the path that will fulfill your potential and bring you success. If you're trying to be someone else, you'll never find your potential and you still won't feel good about yourself because you're not yourself; you're just a copy of someone else.

Healthy self-esteem—legitimately liking and accepting yourself—comes from understanding and embracing your authentic self. It comes from knowing and becoming friends with that person, and treating him or her with all the compassion, respect, and caring you would show your best friend. Only when you know and accept your authentic self, and allow that unique person to grow and flourish, are you able to find real happiness. Believing in and being your authentic self is where your greatest potential lies.

Step 5. **Start building new habits.**

Habits are formed when we repeat something so many times that it becomes automatic—or happens without us consciously thinking about it. For example, when your phone rings, you answer it. You don't have to consciously think, "I hear something ringing; it's my phone; I'll go answer it." You've performed this action so many times that when you hear the ring tone you automatically reach for the phone.

Self-esteem thoughts and behaviors can also become habit. Maybe you sing off-key in chorus and you automatically think negatively: "I'll never get this right; my voice is terrible." Or you automatically think positively: "I have to practice that part more, but I'll get it eventually." Maybe you see a group of kids playing basketball and know you'd like to join in but automatically walk the other way because you assume you'll be rejected. Or you automatically walk toward them and ask if you can play because you believe there's a chance they'll let you.

A habit is actually a connection or pathway set up between your brain cells (or *neurons*). This is called a *neural connection* or *neural pathway*. If you always think negatively when you sing off-key, the connection will form between your singing off-key and negative thoughts. With more repetition this neural connection will strengthen, and your behavior will become automatic: every time you sing off-key, you'll criticize yourself. The same is true for the positive. If you sing off-key and then think positively enough times, that will become your neural connection and your habit.

By the time you're a teen you may have built both negative and positive habits around your self-esteem. The positive habits you'll want to keep, but the negative habits can work against you. Luckily, science tells us our brains are "plastic": they can continue to change, grow, and develop new neural pathways for as long as we live. This means even if a negative habit has become automatic, it's not too late to change. You can change low self-esteem habits to healthy self-esteem habits no matter how long you've had them.

There are four basic steps to changing a habit.

1. *Identify your current automatic behavior.* For example, "When I see a group of kids I'd like to join, I automatically turn around and walk the other way."

2. *Describe the new habit you'd like to build.* "Instead of walking away, I'd like to approach them and say hi."

3. *Catch yourself in the current automatic behavior and make some kind of change.* Any small change in the habit will help shift the automatic pattern. For example, when you notice yourself turning away from the group, you could stop and notice what you're doing before moving on; stop and take a few relaxing breaths before moving on; stop and turn around before moving on; or stop, turn around, and approach them to say hi.

4. *Repeat the change over and over in reality or through visualization.* The more you repeat any part of a

new habit, the sooner the old neural connection will be dismantled in your brain and the new one will take over. You can practice either in the real-life situation, or you can imagine the situation and visualize yourself making the change. Because your brain can't tell the difference between the two, both of these actions are effective. Also, every time you either just observe or make any kind of change in your automatic behavior, you're helping to undo that habit and build a new one.

Step 6. **Practice and repeat, practice and repeat, practice and repeat.**

The key to creating the changes you want is repetition. The more you repeat to yourself that your self-esteem is in your hands, that you have intrinsic value and worth, and that your authentic self is your best self, the sooner those beliefs will become the automatic thoughts you act from that help you build healthy self-esteem. The more you repeat the positive practices in the following pages, the sooner they'll become a natural part of the way you live.

The goal of this book is to help you develop the habits of healthy self-esteem. It will teach you what those habits look like and provide ideas for how to practice them. The book is divided into two parts: Positive Thoughts and Positive Actions. Positive Thoughts provides twenty-five thinking patterns that will help you create and keep a positive perspective about yourself and your life. Positive Actions describes twenty-five behavior choices that stem from wisdom and integrity, producing positive experiences that help you feel good about yourself. All the thought and action activities are intended to keep your self-esteem in your hands, reinforce your intrinsic value and worth, and celebrate your authentic self. They're also designed to be simple and practical enough that you can do them in a relatively short period of time and repeat them over and over.

You'll find each of the fifty activities divided into three sections:

Perceive It describes a particular thought or action and helps you understand how it contributes to healthy self-esteem.

Believe It gives you a positive statement or *affirmation* to read silently or speak aloud that will personalize the idea for you. When you affirm something, you state firmly and positively that it is true. Repeating these affirmations will help your brain start embracing the new ideas.

Achieve It provides an activity to help you start practicing the new thought or action and begin building the healthy self-esteem habit.

Many of the activities suggest that you write out your thoughts or observations or that you make a list. You can do this on paper or electronically or both, whichever feels best for you. Worksheets or templates for some of the activities can be downloaded at the website for this book: http://www.newharbinger.com/39195; you'll find details about this at the back of the book. You may also want to keep a journal so all your writing is contained in one place. Remember that this isn't English class. Nothing you write needs to be seen by anyone else, and you don't have to worry about spelling, punctuation, or grammar. The purpose of writing is simply to record your observations, think something through, or express yourself. Making notes about your thoughts, feelings, observations, and experiences can help you better understand yourself, remember the concepts, and make more progress toward your goals.

Some of the activities suggest you try visualization or guided imagery, which you may or may not be familiar with. As we explained above, imagining a story or an image that illustrates or reinforces your new thoughts or actions helps you rehearse your goal on a neurological level and helps your brain make the changes you want. Many successful athletes, actors, and businesspeople use visualization.

It's important to know that many of these activities will feel good to you but some may not. If some don't click with you, leave them to try again later. When you find those that work best, you can use them over and over. Your old habits were formed by repetition, and your new ones will be, too. The more you practice the healthy self-esteem thoughts and actions, the sooner they'll become automatic and a natural part of who you are. As you practice, remember to do so with self-acceptance instead of judgment. Nonjudgmental observing will help you more than criticism.

Good luck, and enjoy the journey!

the self-esteem habit for teens

positive thoughts

The activities in this section will teach you the thinking habits of healthy self-esteem. When you have healthy self-esteem, you believe in your personal value and worth. You recognize you are in charge of how you think about yourself, and you can choose to view your life in ways that help build your confidence. You generally use a positive perspective, try to see things accurately, and avoid distorting reality. When you find yourself with negative thoughts and feelings, you don't let it throw you into a tailspin; you simply recognize what's happening and then take steps to get back on track again.

The thinking habits that follow are all positive ways of looking at yourself, your life, your place in the universe, and thinking itself. The more you practice these, the more they will become your new habits and build your healthy self-esteem.

1. recognize your power

Ava blamed her father for her low self-esteem. When she was little, he left and never came back. She always wondered if it was because he didn't like her or she wasn't good enough. When she thought this way, she'd feel bad about herself. One day Ava realized her self-esteem could never change as long as she based it on this fictional story. She might never know how her father felt about her, but she didn't have to spend the rest of her life feeling down on herself. She decided to let go of this negative thinking habit, take back her power, and remember that her self-esteem was in her hands, not his.

Perceive It

There can be many circumstances that affect your self-esteem: things that happen, things people say, things you can't control, things you don't like. You might think these things make you feel bad about yourself, and until something changes you can't feel different.

This thinking habit makes you a victim: dependent on something outside yourself to feel okay. In reality, no matter what happens, only you can decide how to think about yourself. When you embrace this power, you can feel good without waiting for circumstances or people to change. When you recognize and accept that your self-esteem is in your hands, you can make a conscious choice of how to think about yourself at any moment. You can choose to see all the good in yourself. You can do this no matter what's happened in the past, what's happening right now, or what happens in the future. When you recognize your power, you can create healthy self-esteem.

Believe It

I am not a victim; my self-esteem is in my hands!

Achieve It

On separate paper or in your journal, make a list of anyone or anything you currently think prevents you from feeling good about yourself. Next, sit quietly and comfortably and take a few relaxing breaths. Close your eyes and imagine yourself standing outdoors on a beautiful day in a location that feels safe to you. Maybe this is a favorite childhood place—a backyard, park, or the shore of a lake or an ocean. Picture yourself smiling and feeling secure. In your hands you're holding stones, each of which represents a person or situation you've given power over your self-esteem. These might be parents, friends, teachers, relatives, or strangers. The circumstances could be divorce, abuse, learning disabilities, finances, emotional or physical handicaps, or anything else. Next, imagine yourself taking one stone from your hand and throwing it far away from you with all your might. You watch the stone fly into the distance, on and on until it disappears. You continue throwing each of the stones purposefully, one at a time, until they're gone. Then take a minute to feel the freedom of letting go. Sit peacefully in this feeling, knowing you've released these influences from your self-esteem. When you're ready, open your eyes and look at your hands, empty of stones. Your self-esteem is in your hands and your control. From now on, only you will decide how you think and feel about yourself.

Remember, your self-concept is just a collection of thoughts about yourself.

—Michael A. Singer

2. claim your value and worth

*Aiden thought of himself as a misfit. He had trouble
managing schoolwork, wasn't coordinated in sports,
and didn't approach people because he was afraid of
rejection. Every day he felt worthless and wondered
why he'd been born. One day when he felt sick and
went to the nurse's office, Miss Hellyer started asking
Aiden about himself. At first he barely replied, but
eventually told her about his poor self-image. "Listen
to me, Aiden," Ms. Hellyer said. "In my thirty years
as a nurse, I've never met a person without value.
You're focusing on surface details and feeding your
bad feelings. Start focusing on the truth: everyone
has value and worth, including you! I don't know
how this thinking habit started, but it's time to stop
or you'll feel miserable the rest of your life."*

Perceive It

Everyone arrives on this planet as an amazing spark of
life with the same intrinsic value and worth. Every infant
is equally significant; each has value; each is a miracle.
You are one of those miracles. No matter where you were

born, what the circumstances of your birth, or whom you were born to, you arrived with value. And just like every other person, you still have it. It doesn't matter what you've said or done or been told—you came in with value and you'll have it the rest of your life. Nothing can change that.

As you grew you may have received and believed messages that caused you to think otherwise. Maybe your hair is straight and someone said wavy is "better." Maybe you love to write poetry and someone said writing poetry is "silly." Maybe you made a mistake and someone said you're "bad." Maybe your caregivers ignored you and you think you're not worthy of attention.

It's essential to remember that nothing can change your intrinsic value. You might make mistakes, be abandoned, get in trouble, or be criticized, but these don't change your innate value and worth. The thinking habit of remembering this truth is a basic foundation for healthy self-esteem.

Believe It

I was born with equal value to every other person on the planet. Nothing I think or say or do can change that fact.

Achieve It

Thought-stopping can help you break a negative thinking habit about your value. To try it, follow these steps:

1. Identify the thoughts you want to eliminate, such as "I'm not good enough," "Everyone's better than me," or "I'm worthless."

2. Choose a word or mental image to help block the thought, such as "Stop!" "No!" or "Halt!" Or use an image of yourself holding up a shield, crossing your arms, zapping the thought with a laser, or something else.

3. When you notice the unwanted thought enter your mind, speak your word strongly (silently or out loud) or bring your image to mind and focus on it intently.

4. Replace the negative thought with a positive one, such as "I am good enough," "I have intrinsic value and worth," or "I reject negative thoughts about my worth."

Note that it's normal for stubborn thoughts to persist and return, but each time you even attempt to stop them, you're breaking the automatic thought cycle and your old thinking habit.

What we must decide is how we are valuable rather than how valuable we are.

—*Edgar Z. Friedenberg*

3. understand and release devaluing messages

Dion's mom suffered from depression and alcohol abuse and never got the help she needed. She had a low stress tolerance and often blamed Dion for her problems, saying it was his fault she struggled so much in life. This wasn't true, but she wasn't healthy enough to see the real origin of her troubles. Dion grew up thinking "I made my mom sick," "I make people feel bad," and "I'm not good enough." A high school counselor finally explained to Dion that his mom's struggles were present long before he was born; he hadn't caused them, but believing that devaluing message was hurting his self-esteem. As Dion worked to release the message and change his thinking habits, he started to feel better about himself.

Perceive It

Our self-esteem develops in great part from both positive and negative messages we receive about ourselves when we're young. For example, you may have heard "You're so good at science," "You'll never amount to anything,"

the self-esteem habit for teens

"You've got a generous heart," or "You should be more like him."

It's important to understand that most caregivers don't intentionally set out to send *devaluing* (damaging) messages. But words can still do harm. Even well-intentioned parents may not realize their negative overtones. They may be speaking from anger or pain, or their own emotional needs may be so unfulfilled that they have little or nothing positive to give to a child.

As a child, you couldn't comprehend this; you just took in everything you heard. You absorbed and believed the messages you received and carried them with you. As a teen, some devaluing messages may still form the base for how you feel about yourself. When you understand their source and that they aren't true, you then have the choice to release them. You can stop the thinking habit of believing devaluing messages and start building healthy self-esteem.

Believe It

I recognize and release any devaluing messages I've received.

Achieve It

On separate paper or in your journal, make a list of any devaluing messages you carry with you, such as "I drive people crazy," "I'm a pain in the neck," "I'm always ruining things," "It's my fault they got divorced," or others. If you can remember, note where each message came from—teachers, parents, relatives, friends, guardians, or acquaintances? Then write a short letter to each of these people, explaining how you understand they didn't mean to hurt you, but their message was damaging and you're going to release it. (Writing this letter is only to help you let go of the message. The goal isn't to criticize the sender, but to work on your own thinking habit. If you think about actually delivering the letter, first talk about this with an adult you trust.) Next, write each devaluing message on a piece of paper and choose a way to destroy it. You might put it through a shredder, tear it into pieces, cut it up, block it out with marker or white-out, tack it to a dartboard and throw darts at it, crumple it up, throw it in the garbage, or do anything else safe and appropriate. As you destroy each one, think or say, "I'm releasing this devaluing message and building new thinking habits of healthy self-esteem."

Accept yourself, love yourself, and keep moving forward. If you want to fly, you have to give up what weighs you down.

—*Roy T. Bennett*

4. choose positive self-messages

Maddie's psychology class was exploring how self-messages affect our lives. Maddie identified some of her self-messages as "I'm a nice girl," "I'm not as smart as my brother," and "I'm good at art." Maddie realized that even though she got good grades, the message "I'm not as smart as my brother" always made her feel bad about herself. She decided to stop comparing herself to her brother and focus on her own strengths. She changed her self-message to "I get good grades and I'm smart enough for me." When she switched to this more positive thinking habit, her self-esteem rose.

Perceive It

Thoughts are constantly flowing through our minds. Those that are observations and judgments about ourselves are called *self-messages*. The self-messages you have today originated partly from what you heard through the years from your family, friends, society, and yourself. Self-messages can be positive or negative and are powerful tools for shaping self-esteem. The more positive self-messages you listen to and believe, the better you'll feel about yourself. The more negative self-messages you listen to and believe, the worse you'll feel about yourself.

As a teen, you have the ability to explore the messages you carry and how they affect you, and release those that are devaluing. You can also make a conscious choice to replace them with new, positive messages that help you feel good about yourself. While no one can control every thought that comes to mind, you can get in the habit of choosing and using positive self-messages to build healthy self-esteem.

Believe It

I don't have to believe or embrace every thought that comes through my mind. I choose and use positive self-messages to help me build healthy self-esteem.

Achieve It

Imagine you are the best parent in the world and you are taking care of yourself as a little child. In your journal or on separate paper, make a list of positive, loving messages you would want to tell yourself as you are growing up. Think about what you needed and wanted to hear as a child. It may have been something like "You are an awesome kid," "I love you so much," "You are skilled and talented," "I love and accept you unconditionally," or "I'm so glad you're my child." Then think about the positive and loving messages you need and want to hear right now as a teen. Maybe these sound like "I'm so proud of you," "It's okay if your grades aren't perfect; I still love you," "I know we're different, but I love and accept you," and so on. Even if no one else is giving you these messages, you can tell them to yourself and reap their benefits. Remember, you create your own self-esteem. Put together all the positive messages you would like to hear about yourself, and make a commitment to read them every day as many times as you're able until you have them memorized. When you instill these positive self-messages in your mind, they'll eventually start appearing automatically whenever you feel disappointed, discouraged, or down on yourself. Claim your power by using these positive self-messages to build your own healthy self-esteem.

Talk to yourself like you would to someone you love.

—Brené Brown

the self-esteem habit for teens

5. adjust your attitude

Destiny felt frustrated and angry at herself. She and Isabella were at a concert, and she'd lost her glasses. She couldn't see well and felt embarrassed searching beneath people's seats. She complained repeatedly about how stupid she was. "I know you're upset," Isabella said, "but you're not stupid. You just misplaced something. Your attitude is ruining the night for both of us. How about thinking positively? Maybe someone will turn in your glasses to the lost and found. In the meantime, enjoy the music. This is our favorite band and we've got great seats." "You're right," Destiny said. "Complaining just makes me feel worse." Destiny changed her attitude and ended up feeling better about herself and having fun.

Perceive It

Attitude is the way we think about things. Adjusting your attitude means thinking about things in a new way. When you choose a positive attitude, you generate positive thoughts; when you choose a negative attitude, you generate negative thoughts. Your attitude determines how you experience every life situation and how you experience yourself. The habit of using a positive attitude is a powerful tool for creating healthy self-esteem.

For example, if you don't make the team and have a negative attitude, you might generate the negative thought, "I'm such a loser; I never do anything right," and you'll feel down on yourself, sad, angry, or helpless. But if you have a positive attitude, you might generate the positive thought, "Oh well, I think I'll try out for the play instead; I'm a good actor," and you'll feel accepting of yourself, hopeful, and content. The good news is, you can always choose which attitude to use.

Believe It

I choose a positive attitude to generate positive thoughts about myself.

Achieve It

Set a glass half-filled with water in front of you and pretend you're extremely thirsty. Imagine you choose a positive attitude and generate positive thoughts about this water, such as "This is great—I've got a half glass of water—just what I need!" Imagine how you feel thinking these positive thoughts. (Happy? Relieved?) Now imagine you choose a negative attitude and generate negative thoughts about this same water, such as "This is terrible—I've only got a half glass of water—that's not enough!" Imagine how you feel now. (Disappointed? Angry?)

Your attitude and your thoughts created either a positive or a negative experience for you. As you go through the day, recognize how you have the ability to adjust your attitude at every moment and create either positive or negative experiences of your life and yourself. When you miss an A by one point, you can think, "I'm smart enough to get that close." When your dad lectures you, you can think, "My dad loves me enough to care what I do." When you're faced with a tough challenge, you can think, "I know I can get through this." Building the habit of choosing a positive attitude toward yourself helps create healthy self-esteem.

Your living is determined not so much by what life brings to you as by the attitude you bring to life; not so much by what happens to you as by the way your mind looks at what happens.

—John Homer Miller

6. practice gratitude

Malik used to be a complainer. He spent a lot of time thinking about how he didn't like his basketball coach, his girlfriend's attitude, his stepdad's rules, his struggle with algebra, or his curly hair. Then his best friend was in a car accident and was in traction. Whenever Malik started complaining, he thought about William and stopped. He realized William would give anything to have these problems instead of his own. When he remembered this, his thoughts changed right to gratitude. He'd tell himself he was grateful to play a sport, spend time with his girlfriend, live at home with rules, go to school, or anything else. When Malik changed his thinking habit from complaining to gratitude, he became happier with his life and himself.

Perceive It

Gratitude is an attitude of thankfulness and appreciation. When you think with an attitude of gratitude, you put your attention on everything good in your life and yourself. You concentrate on all you have instead of what you think you're missing. You put a spotlight on everything favorable and strengthen positive thinking habits.

You can feel grateful for the biggest to the smallest things: a smile from someone, your breakfast, your family, your home, your fingernails, your skill at golf, your ability to get up from a chair and walk. During times of loss or sadness, it's harder to feel grateful, but if you look deep enough, there's always something to be thankful for. Focusing your thoughts on gratitude gets your brain in the habit of seeing the good in everything, including yourself, which builds healthy self-esteem.

Believe It

I focus on the good in my life and myself; there is always something to be grateful for.

Achieve It

Set an intention to immerse yourself in gratitude today. When you wake up, start keeping track of everything good. The first thing can be the fact you woke up. Do you have a pillow? Add that. Can you swallow? Add that. Can you get out of bed on your own? Add that. Challenge yourself to find fifty good things and record them in your journal or on separate paper. When you reach fifty, go for one hundred. When you hit one hundred, keep going.

Remember to include positives about yourself: you helped your mom by taking out the garbage, you gave your sister a hug, you remembered your homework, you passed the quiz, you got to practice on time, you listened to your friend's problems. When something happens you view as "bad," your brain might jump right to "This isn't fair," or "I'm so stupid." Start a new neural connection to change that habit by choosing a thought of gratitude. Find something good about your life or yourself. Then find another, and another, until your negative thoughts are gone. At the end of each day, carefully read over your list. When these are your last thoughts before falling asleep, you'll instill the thinking habit of gratitude and build healthy self-esteem.

We think that people are grateful because they are happy. But is this true? Look closely, and you will find that people are happy because they are grateful.

—David Steindl-Rast

the self-esteem habit for teens

7. celebrate your strengths

Natalie was admiring all the trophies and blue ribbons in Jayla's room. "Wow, you're good at so much," she said. "I'm terrible at all these things; I've never won an award." "They just don't give trophies for the things you're good at," said Jayla. "What do you mean?" asked Natalie. "Your strengths are visible all year-round, not just in certain seasons or competitions," Jayla answered. "The trophies you'd get would be for being an incredible person. We all know we can tell you anything and you'll keep it quiet, you'd come running if we ever needed help, and you never talk behind our backs. Stop thinking about what you can't do and remember that strengths come in all different forms—yours are the qualities everyone wants in a friend."

Perceive It

Everyone has flaws, frailties, and weaknesses but we also all have strengths. If we spend more time thinking about the areas we *don't* excel in, we paint unrealistically negative pictures of ourselves. Dwelling on our imperfections makes our neural pathways grow stronger for seeing vulnerabilities and weaker for recognizing things we could be celebrating. This thinking habit lowers our self-esteem.

You might think that you have far more weaknesses than strengths or that you don't have any strengths at all. This is a false belief. If you're alive, you have strengths; there's no person without them. Your strengths might be physical, like being good at field hockey, tai chi, cooking, or horseback riding; or intellectual, like excelling at chemistry, computer science, or problem solving. They might be emotional, like staying calm in a crisis, showing compassion, or having patience. Maybe your strengths are being generous, organized, loyal, hardworking, or reliable, or expressing yourself clearly. When you build the thinking habit of focusing on and celebrating the things you're good at and the qualities you're proud of, you'll build healthy self-esteem.

Believe It

I focus on my strengths and my best qualities to build a positive attitude about myself.

Achieve It

Make headings for the following categories on separate paper or in your journal: Emotional, Intellectual, Physical, Creative. You can also download a blank chart at http://www.newharbinger.com/39195. Then take a breath, clear your mind of past judgments, and list your personal strengths under each category. The sample lists include possibilities for each category.

Emotional

generosity

perseverance

courage

kind-heartedness

positivity

Intellectual

reading

math

research

brainstorming

chemistry

Physical

soccer

flexibility

softball

karate

badminton

balance

nutrition

Creative

playing trombone

interior design

cartooning

sculpting

writing

planning parties

List every strength from the smallest to the biggest. If you have trouble, think about what other people would tell you, or ask someone you trust for an opinion. Often other people can see your strengths more clearly than you can. After each item listed, write at least one example of a specific time you exhibited this strength. Finally, read over what you've written. Remember, these strengths don't make you better than anyone else, but they are real and they are yours. Look at them regularly to build the habit of thinking positively about yourself.

I am larger, better than I thought, I did not know I held so much goodness.

—*Walt Whitman*

8. embrace your differences

Michael hated his sensitivity. Most of his friends liked horror films and contact sports, but Michael preferred happy endings and working out solo. He didn't like that his feelings ran deep and that he took things to heart. His self-esteem suffered because he thought he should be like everyone else. One day his girlfriend told him he needed to stop worrying and see that his sensitivity was a gift. "That's why I like you," she said. "You care about my feelings and are a better boyfriend because of it. That's why you're going to be a great writer someday because you notice subtle details in life, you feel below the surface, and you recognize other people's trials and longings. Stop thinking you should be like everyone else; your differences are valuable."

Perceive It

Our survival in this universe is dependent on differences. We need bees and locusts just as much as giraffes and owls; leafy plants as much as cactus; and rainstorms as much as hot, sunny days. We also need differences in the human race to meet all its needs. Dentists, farmers, teachers, machinists, homemakers, computer technologists and all others play roles in keeping our planet running.

When you embrace your differences, you accept them and see the good in them. You don't feel ashamed or embarrassed of the ways you stand out or stand apart from others. You know there is a perfect place for you on this planet because of your uniqueness. Instead of feeling bad about yourself because of the ways you're different, you celebrate those differences and use them to create an amazing life for yourself, touching others and the world in a positive way. Embracing your differences builds healthy self-esteem.

Believe It

My differences are valuable; they contribute something important to my life and to the world.

Achieve It

Imagine you're at the grocery store or an all-you-can-eat-buffet. Picture all the colors, shapes, sizes, textures, and tastes of the multitude of different foods. Then imagine what it would be like if instead of hundreds of choices there were only one: only one type of food in the grocery store; only one food to eat for breakfast, lunch, and dinner;

only one food at the buffet. This is an example of a world without differences.

Next, on separate paper or in your journal, make a list of the traits that make you different or unique—these could be "I have a crazy sense of humor," "I'm adventurous," "I'm quiet," "I think outside the box," "I'm steady when others are off balance," or any other character trait of yours. Describe the ways your differences benefit you, your family, your friend group, your school or community, and the world. The habit of seeing your differences in a positive light will create healthy self-esteem and help you bring your unique talents to others.

Differences should be seen as strengths, not weaknesses. They add zest to life.

—Stephen Covey

9. view yourself with compassion

*Matthew's science project on passive solar design
looked great, but he'd gotten some major facts wrong
in his research and would have to do part of it over.
He felt really embarrassed after his presentation and
told himself he was stupid for messing up like this. His
science teacher thought differently. "Matthew, you're
being really hard on yourself; have a little compassion.
You tackled a tough subject and did a decent job. Beating
yourself up won't help you do better next time. Give
yourself some credit for all the work you did and be a
little kinder; then you'll have the energy to start again."*

Perceive It

Compassion is a deep sympathy or caring for any living
creature who is suffering. The habit of viewing yourself
with compassion means you think about yourself from
a perspective of understanding and kindness instead of
faultfinding and criticism. If you notice something you
don't like about yourself or if you're feeling vulnerable,
you approach yourself with a warm and gentle attitude.

Many of us are good at seeing others with compassion but are harder on ourselves. Where you might think kindly of someone else who has made a mistake or is hurting, you think of yourself more harshly and are less forgiving. But condemning and shaming yourself only lead to negativity, anxiety, and despair instead of positive change or growth. Compassion is a helpful, supportive, and accepting attitude that reinforces your intrinsic value, generates positive thoughts about yourself, and creates a calm, secure base from which to move forward.

Believe It

I approach myself with compassion and kindness to maintain a positive attitude and build healthy self-esteem.

Achieve It

Think about what compassion sounds like. On separate paper or in your journal, make a list of kind words you would say to a friend who feels anxious, a child who's crying, or someone who's sick. They might sound something like "I'm sorry you're feeling this way," "It'll turn out all right," "You'll feel better soon," or "I'm here for you." Then identify a current situation in your life where you need to see yourself with compassion. Write a dialogue between the compassionate part of you and the hurting part of you, using some of the words, phrases, or statements you might use for a friend. For example, your dialogue might sound like this:

"What's wrong?"

"I got fired from my job. I'm such an idiot."

"Hey, don't be so hard on yourself. You're not an idiot; you just made a mistake."

"But it was a big one."

"I know, but it's okay. You're a good person, and you can do better next time. There are other jobs. I believe in you."

"Talking" to yourself like this might feel awkward at first, but try it anyway. Cruel self-criticism will only make you feel worse about yourself. Seeing yourself with compassion is a thinking habit that fosters healthy self-esteem.

You've been criticizing yourself for years and it hasn't worked. Try approving of yourself and see what happens.

—Louise L. Hay

10. learn from your mistakes

Kanan read the recipe wrong in cooking class and forgot to put sugar in his brownies. They tasted pretty bad, and Kanan felt embarrassed and down on himself. "I can't believe I did that," he said. "Who makes brownies without sugar?" "It's okay," the teacher said. "We all make mistakes; just figure out what you've learned and make another batch in the next class." "I learned I need to read the ingredient list more carefully," Kanan said. "Next time I'll check off each one as I add it." Kanan's second batch turned out great. "These are excellent," the teacher said. "Now focus on what you learned and how you fixed things instead of what you did wrong; then let it go and enjoy your brownies!"

Perceive It

There are delete keys on every keyboard for a reason: mistakes are a normal part of life. But when we see our mistakes negatively, we create negative thoughts about ourselves. Sometimes we even dwell on mistakes, berating ourselves over and over for doing something wrong. This thinking habit tears down self-esteem.

Looking at mistakes with a positive attitude helps you transcend them. As the story goes, when Thomas Edison tried over 900 times to create a working light bulb, someone asked him how he felt about his failures. Edison said, "I didn't fail—I just found 899 ways not to make a light bulb." When you make a mistake, choose Edison's thinking habit and see the positive. This perspective helps create healthy self-esteem.

Believe It

I learn from mistakes, fix them, and then let them go instead of dwelling on what I did wrong.

Achieve It

When you focus on how you fix your mistakes, you can feel good about yourself for learning something new and making corrections. This is the positive thinking habit that builds healthy self-esteem. The next time you make a mistake, try doing the following:

1. Identify what you can learn from it. For example, if you said something rude, you might need to think more before you speak. If you dropped

the self-esteem habit for teens

your books, you might need to carry fewer at one time. If you did your math homework wrong, you might need to study more.

2. Do what you can to fix it. If you said something rude, apologize; if you dropped your books, pick them up; if you did the math wrong, find out how to do it right and do it over.

3. Stop thinking about it. Let it go from your mind and move on to the next moment of your life.

Mistakes are the portals of discovery.

—James Joyce

11. compare to yourself, not to others

Jonathan watched the other guys at the skate park and felt embarrassed. He had nowhere near the skill level they did; he fell twice as often and couldn't do half the tricks. He felt like a loser and wondered whether he should even bother to try anymore. As he was heading for home, one of the most talented skaters called to him. "Hey," Derek said. "I can't believe how much you've improved this summer! I wish I'd caught on that fast when I started." "Really?" Jonathan said. "I thought I was doing terribly compared to you guys." "Don't compare to us," Derek said. "We've been skating way longer than you. Compare to yourself; you're doing great."

Perceive It

Comparing ourselves to other people can damage healthy self-esteem because it makes us feel good or bad about ourselves based someone else's life experience. All our journeys are different, and we progress in different ways at different rates; where we are is right for us no matter what's happening with others. There will always be those with greater talent than ours and those with lesser; this doesn't make them either "better" or "not as good" as us. Our value doesn't change just because we compare.

If you're in ninth grade and compare your reading skills to a third grader's, you'll feel falsely superior. If you compare to a college student, you'll feel falsely inferior. To feel good about yourself, compare to yourself. Think back a year or six months, and look for any improvements you've made since then, even if they're small. Measure by your direction: are you moving forward over time? Focusing on your own progress and growth in your own life is a thinking habit that creates healthy self-esteem.

Believe It

When I want an accurate reading of my progress, I compare myself to myself, not to others.

Achieve It

Identify two goals you've achieved since you were born, and record them on separate paper or in your journal. These could be learning to spell, playing a drum solo, winning an award for archery, or anything else. Then make a time line showing your path to achieving each of these goals. For example, your drumming time line might look like this: "age 2—started banging pots and pans on the kitchen floor; age 5—played a toy drum concert for grandparents; age 9—started drum lessons; age 12—played drums in the school band; age 14—had first drum solo." If at age fourteen you feel frustrated that your drum skills aren't as good as a rock star's or even others in your grade, stop comparing to them and look back at your own progress to compare to yourself. Feel good about how you've kept moving forward.

Next, choose something you're currently working toward and make a time line to show your progress so far. Keep this time line on hand until you achieve your goal, and remember to compare to yourself instead of someone else to build healthy self-esteem.

Never compare yourself to anyone else, only to your own previous best.

—*Ric Alexander*

12. love your body

Brianna was bigger than any girl and most boys in her class. She was tall and large-boned and felt like a giant. She tried to slouch and eat less to become smaller but nothing worked, and every day she hated the way she looked. One day the swim coach approached her. "Why don't you celebrate your body instead of berating it?" Ms. Clark asked. "Long, strong arms and legs can really move through water." Brianna joined the swim team and began breaking records. She stopped worrying about how her body compared to others and became grateful for it instead.

Perceive It

We come into the world loving our bodies, fascinated by how our legs kick and fingers wiggle. Then we hear messages that say bodies are valuable only if they look a certain way. These are arbitrary opinions that change through the decades. In ancient Greece, it was important for the distance between nipples and navel to be equal. In legendary actress Marilyn Monroe's time, voluptuous curves were valued. Some years males "should" be lean, other times bulging with muscle.

Having healthy self-esteem means you recognize that all bodies are different and are supposed to be that way. You stop thinking negatively about this awesome machine and start loving your body for the miracle it is. You appreciate the "mobile home" that carries you wherever you want to go, lets you water-ski, sleep, taste pizza, rock climb, hug, kiss, laugh, curl up on the couch, and see a sunset. When you change the thinking habit of criticizing your body to appreciating all that's right with it, your self-esteem can grow.

Believe It

I love my body for all the amazing gifts it brings me.

Achieve It

Do something positive for yourself and your body: Lie down comfortably where you won't be disturbed. Put on some soft music if you'd like. Close your eyes and take several peaceful breaths. Feel the air moving in and out of your body and let your muscles relax. Know you are safe and secure. Then, starting with the top of your head and moving slowly down to the tips of your toes, focus on each body part one at a time with a loving attitude. Think about how each part has helped you and the gifts it has brought you. For example, your eyes have helped you see beauty in the world, move without bumping into things, connect with loved ones, and release stress through tears. Your stomach has sent you signals when you're hungry, broken down foods, and processed the nutrients you need to live. Your legs have helped you move from place to place, climb trees, swing on swings, ride your bike, run relays, and dance to your favorite music. You may have criticized your body parts before, dwelling on what you didn't like or how you wished they were different. Undo that negative thinking habit by honoring every body part and sending it love and kindness. Feel how each muscle, bone, and cell responds to this positive care. Set the intention to stop believing unrealistic ideals about how your body should look and focus on the positive realities instead.

There's nothing wrong with your body, but there's a lot wrong with the messages that try and convince you otherwise.

—Rae Smith

13. see infinite possibilities

All year Julie planned to get a summer job so she could save money for a car. She really wanted to become more self-reliant. Then her parents said she'd have to babysit her little brother instead. Julie felt angry and disappointed, telling herself she'd never be independent. "Don't think so narrowly," her friend Maya said. "Look for more possibilities. Maybe you could work from home. You're so good at math and tech stuff; you could tutor kids or help people set up their computers or design websites—or all three! Open your mind—you're not as limited as you think. There's more than one way to become independent and feel good about yourself."

Perceive It

When we limit our range of thinking, we limit ourselves, our lives, and our self-esteem. Many of us view life using tunnel vision, realizing only a small portion of what exists and what is possible. When you practice opening your mind and expanding your thinking, you open up a world of potential. Viewing life with a limited scope makes you feel stuck and helpless in both your outer circumstances and your feelings about yourself. Broadening that scope brings empowerment, hope, and joy.

It's very rare that anyone is truly stuck, although you may think you are. In reality, there are always options and opportunities beyond what you see at first glance. When you get in the habit of seeing the infinite possibilities in every moment, situation, and person, including yourself, you can grow, change, and become anything you desire. You create successes and build healthy self-esteem.

Believe It

I can see beyond just what's in front of me. There are infinite possibilities in every moment and in myself.

Achieve It

Practice stretching your thoughts to see infinite possibilities. Choose one or more of these objects: ring, spoon, book, shoe, football, facial tissue, teddy bear, hammer, pillow, blender, orange, leaf. Purposely open your mind, and on separate paper or in your journal, list all possible uses you can think of for this item; you can also download a worksheet at http://www.newharbinger.com/39195. For example, you could use a ring to play catch with, hang in a window, or trace circles with. You could use a spoon as a bookmark, balance it on your nose, or dig in the dirt with it. Try to list ten ideas for each item; if you can, keep going. Next, use the same method to find solutions for a current challenge. If you write, "best friend angry and won't talk to me," possible solutions could be: call her, apologize, get peer counseling, ask parents to intervene, send a card, give her some time, write her a song, fix what I did wrong, send a gift, go out for coffee, cry, make a date to talk, move on and find a new friend, and so on. Finally, open your mind and find new ways to think about yourself to build healthy self-esteem. For example, if you write, "I'm too shy," you could open to "I'm just right for me," "There's nothing wrong with being shy," "I'm actually not shy around everyone," "If I really want to, I can work on social skills and interact more." Remember, thinking you're stuck keeps you stuck. The thinking habit of seeing possibilities opens up opportunities for anything you want.

In this moment, there is plenty of time. In this moment, you are precisely as you should be. In this moment, there is infinite possibility.

—*Victoria Moran*

the self-esteem habit for teens

14. focus on the present moment

Emma had a hard time letting go of negative thoughts about herself. She obsessed about Margaret liking Alyssa more than her, about her haircut looking bad, about a comment she made that someone took the wrong way. Emma's stress level went up and her self-esteem went down because she kept getting stuck in her negative thinking habit. She finally changed this habit by practicing mindfulness, or focusing her attention on the present moment. This helped her let go of negative self-thoughts one moment at a time. The more Emma practiced mindfulness, the more she could let go of any negative thoughts that came up and the better she felt about herself.

Perceive It

Mindfulness is the thinking practice of paying attention to the present moment without judgment. It means briefly separating from the thoughts spinning through your mind and just observing what's happening here and now. You notice what's happening inside and outside you without getting caught up in it. Mindfulness strengthens your "focus muscle" and helps your brain practice leaving distraction and returning to peace. It also helps you let go of your inner critic. When you practice mindfulness, you try observing just what actually is.

Focusing on the present moment instead of on negative self-thoughts can help build healthier self-esteem. For example, if you're berating yourself for something you did wrong yesterday, you can notice those thoughts without judgment, let them pass, and come back to the present moment. If you walk by two people who are laughing and think, "They're making fun of me," you can notice and release that thought and focus on where you're going. This practice breaks your negative thinking pattern. Then you can choose a different thought, such as "They must have heard a good joke." Over time, the mindfulness habit helps your brain get unstuck from the negative thinking that damages self-esteem.

Believe It

Mindfulness helps me let go of negative thoughts by keeping my focus on the present moment.

Achieve It

Try mindfulness right now, using your five senses to focus on the moment. For example, as you read, notice the words, ink color, and shapes of the letters. Notice whether whatever you're touching feels smooth or rough, warm or cool. Notice the sounds and smells around you and any taste in your mouth. Observe which parts of your body feel comfortable and which don't. Notice your emotions: are you content, bored, angry, curious, happy, annoyed, or anything else? Try to observe without judgment; just see what is and let it be.

Practice mindfulness at any time; while you're brushing your teeth, walking, watching TV, or listening to music, just keep your attention on that one activity. In class, notice how the teacher looks, what he's saying, the notes you're taking. Running laps, notice the beat of your heart, pounding of your feet, strength of your muscles, air on your face. When talking with friends, really hear what they're saying, and see their expressions, body language, emotions. Build the mindfulness habit by choosing regular times to tune in to the present moment, such as whenever the phone rings, you take a drink, open a door, or notice a negative self-thought. Set an intention now to practice mindfulness at least once in the next twenty-four hours.

If you want to conquer the anxiety of life, live in the moment, live in the breath.

—Amit Ray

15. avoid overgeneralizing

Sam asked someone to a dance and was turned down. "No one will ever go out with me," he concluded. He asked for fries and was given onion rings by mistake. "My order always gets messed up," he thought. He told his counselor he might drop out of school because he failed a class. "I'll never graduate," he said. His counselor called him out on his distorted thinking habit. "You need to watch your thoughts," she said. "If you keep overgeneralizing, you'll end up depressed and lonely. It's time to start looking at the facts and thinking rationally if you ever want to feel good about yourself."

Perceive It

Overgeneralizing is a distorted thinking habit. It makes use of words like "always," "never," "all," "none," "no one," and "everyone." Distorted-thinking statements are inaccurate perceptions of reality. For example, if you fail two out of four history tests and say, "I always fail my history tests," this is an overgeneralization; it's not true. The reality is you took four tests, passed two, and failed two. When you process the facts with an overgeneralized bias, you're distorting reality.

Overgeneralizing can damage your self-esteem because you interpret things as worse than they really are. If you're rejected by one person and think, "No one likes me," you'll feel bad about yourself based on a false statement. Changing the thinking habit of overgeneralizing to one of more accurate thinking can help you build healthier self-esteem.

Believe It

I stop myself from overgeneralizing and look at the facts instead.

Achieve It

To better understand overgeneralizing, stand in front of a regular mirror. What you see in front of you accurately reflects reality. The arms, legs, and head in the mirror look just like the arms, legs, and head on your actual body. This mirror is like clear thinking—it's accurate. Now imagine you're standing in front of a funhouse mirror. When you look into this mirror, your vision of yourself is distorted. You might look taller, shorter, wider, or narrower than you really are. You might even look wavy or broken up. Funhouse mirrors distort reality: what you see is not what's real. In a similar way, overgeneralizing distorts reality: when you overgeneralize you think things are different than they actually are. For example, when someone turns you down for a job, clear thinking tells you "This person turned me down," but overgeneralized thinking tells you "Everyone always turns me down."

If you believe overgeneralized statements about yourself, you'll damage your self-esteem. You can change this thinking habit by paying close attention to your use of words such as "never," "always," "no one," and "everyone" in relation to yourself. When you hear yourself using these words, picture the funhouse mirror and remember that these statements don't accurately reflect you—they're not real. The more you pair these words with a funhouse mirror image, the more you'll connect the two in your mind. You'll start thinking of overgeneralizing as distorted reality and have an easier time breaking this thinking habit.

A problem is as big as you make it. Don't overgeneralize and say the problem reflects your entire life.

—David J. Abbott, MD

16. don't take everything personally

When Meggie leaves a message for Aisha and Aisha doesn't call her back right away, Meggie starts to wonder what's wrong. She tells herself Aisha is mad at her or trying to avoid her. She wonders if Aisha doesn't want to be friends anymore and worries Aisha will tell others that Meggie isn't fun or caring. Meggie's self-esteem is affected negatively by her thinking. When Rylee leaves a message for Aisha and Aisha doesn't call her back right away, Rylee doesn't take it personally or worry. She tells herself Aisha is probably busy and will get back to her when she has time. Rylee goes on with her life, and her self-esteem remains intact.

Perceive It

Healthy self-esteem means you understand that other people's thoughts and actions aren't always related to you, so you don't take everything personally. For example, if your cousin doesn't comment on your new jacket, it doesn't have to mean she doesn't like it; it might mean she's distracted by an argument she just had with her parents. If you're not invited to join your friend to watch a movie, it doesn't have to mean he's mad at you; it might mean he just wants some time alone.

When you believe that every time someone ignores you or is impolite to you it's because there's something wrong with you, you'll feel bad about yourself your whole life. All people have daily personal challenges that distract them and consume their time and energy. They carry their own needs and concerns with them, just as you do. If you're worrying about your grandfather's illness and forget to meet your friends at the mall, it's because issues in your family life overshadowed your social life. Your friends shouldn't take it personally or think you're mad at them.

Sometimes it's true that words and actions are meant directly for you, but not all the time. If you can release the thinking habit of taking everything personally, you can avoid this misperception and feel better about yourself more of the time.

Believe It

I check things out before taking words or actions personally because I know they aren't always about me.

Achieve It

The next time someone does or says something that you take personally, and you feel your self-esteem dip, ask yourself these questions to keep that thinking habit from taking hold:

Do I know for sure this was a personal comment or action toward me?

What is my proof that it was meant personally?

What are at least two other possible reasons this could have been done or said that are not personal?

If I asked two other people, would they agree this was meant personally?

Is there someone else I can check this out with?

Am I willing to check it out with the person who said or did it?

Even if you never find out for sure how the words or actions were meant, going through this question list will help you break the automatic thinking habit of taking everything personally and help you maintain healthy self-esteem.

There is a huge amount of freedom that comes to you when you take nothing personally.

—*Don Miguel Ruiz*

17. believe in abundance

Luis had a hard time sharing other people's triumphs because he thought they threatened his own chances for success. When Ayana's essay got chosen for the school magazine, Luis felt jealous and worried, and his self-esteem dipped. How would he ever become known as a good writer with Ayana doing it so well? When Joshua got a date for the winter dance, Luis felt bad about himself again. What if there was no one left to go with him? Finally, Joshua called him out on it. "As long as you think other people's successes are going to take away from yours, you're going to feel bad, Luis. You've got to relax; there's plenty for everyone!"

Perceive It

Most of us have either a "scarcity" or an "abundance" mind-set. Those with a scarcity mind-set worry that there isn't enough in the world to go around—that includes physical resources like food, clothing, shelter, and money, as well as emotional resources such as love and well-being. They feel jealous or worried if someone else has what they want, whether that's a car, a hairstyle, or a friend. They think because another person has it, there won't be any for them. This thinking habit creates a victim mentality and closes them off from other people.

On the other hand, when you carry an *abundance* mindset, you believe the universe is full and holds enough for everyone. You rejoice in other people's triumphs without feeling cheated, because you know your own needs will be met as well. You consciously focus on abundance and realize that just because you don't have something now doesn't mean you won't get it later. When you're an abundance thinker, you practice gratitude and positive thinking, easily share what you have, feel good about yourself and others, and are more pleasant and fun to be around. You also create healthier self-esteem.

Believe It

There is plenty for everyone; I can get what I need and be happy when others do, too.

Achieve It

Scientists estimate there are one billion trillion stars in the observable universe and five hundred quadrillion grains of sand on our planet. Set up a visual reminder of abundance by filling a bowl, jar, or other container with grains of sand, salt, or sugar; poppy, sesame, or other seeds; glitter, sequins, peppercorns, cake sprinkles, small beads, or something similar. Set this where you can see it regularly, and keep an additional supply of your filling on hand. When someone sees your abundance bowl, offer to share some. Give away your items frequently and refill your bowl again. Create an affirmation such as "I have everything I need," or "Everything I need comes to me," or "There is plenty for all of us." When you notice yourself in a scarcity mind-set, repeat your affirmation over and over. Affirm that you'll get everything you need when you need it, just like everyone else.

When you realize there is nothing lacking, the whole world belongs to you.

—Lao-tzu

the self-esteem habit for teens

18. see the bigger picture

Hailey had a part in the chorus for the school musical. She loved being in theater and working with the whole cast and crew to put on a production. On opening night, Hailey did a wrong turn as part of a dance number and knocked down another chorus member. They were in the back row and the girl got into place again quickly, so not many people noticed, but Hailey felt terrible. She replayed the scene in her mind for hours, which made her feel down on herself and think about quitting the show. "You've got to shake this off," the director said. "It was a small mistake, Hailey. You did a great job in all the other numbers. Stop focusing on this one flaw and see the bigger picture. You're an asset to the show, and we want you in it." Hailey realized she'd been ignoring the facts that the rest of the show had gone well. When she thought from a bigger perspective, she did feel better.

Perceive It

Focusing on one small negative aspect of a situation can damage self-esteem. A healthier thinking habit is to see the bigger picture, or realize that a detail is always just one part of a bigger unit and often insignificant when seen in comparison to the whole.

For example, if you knock over your drink while you're on a date, you might feel embarrassed, but dwelling on that two-second event and judging yourself as klutzy or awkward because of it can send your self-esteem downward. However, if you see that event as one small part of the whole date, you can remind yourself that the rest of the night you got along well together, enjoyed the movie and dinner, and felt good about your connection with the other person. The thinking habit of focusing on the bigger picture provides a more accurate perspective and helps you feel better about yourself.

Believe It

I view things as parts of a bigger picture and know my mistakes and mishaps are minor occurrences in relation to the whole.

Achieve It

On a small piece of paper, write something negative you've been focusing on that makes you feel bad about yourself. Take a close-up picture of this paper so your writing covers the whole photograph. Then put the small paper somewhere in the middle of your bedroom. Move farther away, and take a picture of the entire room with the small paper in the middle. Look at both pictures side by side, and see how big your negative writing looks when it's the whole picture and how much smaller it looks when you see it in the bigger picture, as just one small part of your room. The same thing happens when you mentally focus on one problem close up compared to seeing it in the bigger picture of your life. The next time you find yourself overfocusing on a small detail and feeling bad about yourself, change that thinking habit to seeing the bigger picture and help yourself build healthy self-esteem.

If you just focus on the smallest details, you never get the big picture right.

—Leroy Hood

19. eliminate all-or-nothing thinking

Francisco was trying to get fit before the wrestling season started. He spent his afternoons in the weight room, lifting and doing pull-ups, sit-ups, and push-ups. He also tried eating better, with protein drinks, and fresh fruits and vegetables. One day he had a large ice cream sundae with his friends and then didn't have as good a workout. "I stink at training!" he said, feeling down on himself. "You don't stink," his coach said. "You're great at training. You had one dish of ice cream; now just go back to your healthy eating plan. Stop the all-or-nothing thinking so you can feel good about yourself again."

Perceive It

All-or-nothing is a thinking habit where we see things in extremes or "black-and-white" categories. This thought pattern is illogical because in reality things are never completely one way or the other. Life situations and people's characters and actions generally fall in a "gray" area, somewhere in the middle of two extremes. When you use the all-or-nothing habit to think about yourself, you view yourself incorrectly and your self-esteem suffers. For example, if you head the dance committee, run short on refreshments, and then think, "I'm a terrible party planner," you'll feel bad about yourself based on a falsehood. You aren't a terrible planner; you just made a mistake in estimating. If you're generally a good baby-sitter, but one night can't get the kids to bed on time and think, "I'm no good with children," you'll feel down on yourself unnecessarily. You're still good with children; you just had an off night. All-or-nothing thinking hurts your self-esteem because you label yourself a failure for making one mistake. Healthy self-esteem involves recognizing and accepting that reality lies in the area between extremes.

Believe It

I don't think about myself in all-or-nothing terms because those extremes aren't real.

Achieve It

Help your brain shift from all-or-nothing to a realistic thinking habit. On one sticky note, describe how you perform an activity in one extreme; for example, "I am the perfect debater." On a second sticky note, write the opposite extreme: "I mess up every point and stumble over every word in every debate I'm in." Then do the same with two or more other activities, such as "I'm the best friend who ever existed" and "I'm the worst friend on the planet" or "I'm 100 percent fluent every time I use sign language" and "I make every sign incorrectly whenever I use sign language." In your bedroom or another room, stick one page of your sticky-note pair on one wall and the other on the opposite wall. Then stand in the place between the two extremes that best represents the truth. (If you make mistakes in debate 50 percent of the time, stand right in the middle. Or, stand closer or further to whichever extreme is most accurate.) Remember the physical image of this gray area to help you choose more realistic thoughts the next time you use all-or-nothing thinking.

Don't use all-or-nothing thinking. Take each day as its own day, and don't worry about it if you mess up one day. The most important thing you can do is just get back up on the horse.

—Henry Cloud

20. realize no one has a perfect life

Grace always dreaded visits with her cousin Abigail, because just being in her presence made Grace feel bad about herself. Abigail had the best grades, most popular friends, and prettiest clothes, and was always winning awards for something. "It's not fair," Grace told her mom. "Abigail is flawless." "Grace," her mom said, "did you know Abigail ran away from home twice last year? She's not a happy girl, and she doesn't know how to cope well. Things aren't always what they seem from the outside."

Perceive It

Believing that someone else's life is better, happier, or easier than ours is a thinking habit that lowers self-esteem. These thoughts can occur because we see only a fraction of other people's lives from the outside. If the fraction we see looks better than ours, we feel bad. If we could see their whole lives in detail, however, we'd discover the things about themselves and their lives they don't like. No human has a perfect life. Knowing one thing a person did Friday night, watching a three-minute video clip of her, or seeing her talking to others from a distance doesn't tell us what her private challenges are.

The saying "The grass is always greener on the other side of the fence" illustrates this fact. If you're looking at other people's lawns from far away, you can't see all the weeds and bare spots—just like they can't see yours from over there. While their grass might seem greener, it's really not. When you change the thinking habit that someone else has it better to knowing that everyone has struggles, you can feel better about yourself.

Believe It

Every human being has challenges, even if I can't see them from the outside.

Achieve It

Identify the item farthest away in your view right now. It might be a cloud, a building, a picture on a far wall, or something in the back of your closet. Count how many details of this item you can see. Now imagine you've shortened the distance between you and that item by half. How many details could you see now? What if you were an inch away—how many would you see then? It's the same item you first viewed from far away, but with more information you get a more accurate idea of what it's really like.

The same is true with other people's lives. On separate paper or in your journal, make a list of people "on the other side of your fence," whose lives you think look so much better. Then imagine you know what happens in their houses at night, what they write in their diaries, or what they feel when they're alone. After each name, list any possible challenges that person might have that aren't visible from the outside. These might involve academics, family, health, friends, emotions, job, activities, self-esteem, or anything else. As you go through the day, notice times you think you see greener grass and remind yourself that from where others are, your grass looks greener, too.

The reason we struggle with insecurity is because we compare our behind the scenes with someone else's highlight reel.

—*Steven Furtick*

21. think from the facts, not the feeling

Hannah felt angry and hurt when her friends called her from a party on Saturday night. "They knew I couldn't go. They just wanted to rub it in that they were having fun and I was home studying," she told her dad. These thoughts made her feel dejected and down on herself. "Do you know for sure that's a fact?" her dad asked. "Or do you just feel hurt and left out? Is it possible they were missing you and wanted to cheer you up because you couldn't be with them?" Hannah started to protest but then considered what her father had said. The facts were that her friends had never been mean to her before and earlier they had shown disappointment that she couldn't go to the party. When she considered the facts instead of just her feelings, Hannah realized that maybe her dad was right.

Perceive It

When you draw conclusions based on your feelings instead of the facts of a situation, you're using the thinking habit of *emotional reasoning*. You're viewing your feelings as evidence of the way things really are, even though this isn't true. This thinking pattern distorts reality and causes you to react to things that aren't actually happening; for example, you might feel lonely and believe it's because no one wants to be friends with you, or you might feel bored and believe you're a boring person.

It's important to note the difference between feelings and facts. A feeling is an emotional experience, such as "disappointed," "happy," or "annoyed." A fact is something backed up by evidence that can't be disputed, such as "I have black hair." Thinking from your feelings can cause you to judge yourself negatively, damaging your self-esteem. For example, if you feel rejected and think, "People don't like me," you'll feel bad about yourself. When you look for evidence of that, however, you'll probably realize there are people in your life who want to be with you and be your friends. Just because you're feeling something doesn't mean it's true.

Believe It

I draw conclusions based on facts, not on feelings.

Achieve It

To change an emotional reasoning thinking habit, ask yourself these questions:

1. "Is this a fact or a feeling?"

   For example, if you return to your bleacher seat to find your friends gone and you feel abandoned, stop and think clearly. Is it true that they've abandoned you or do you just feel that way? If you realize it's probably not true, remind yourself that your thinking is distorting reality.

2. "What's my evidence?"

   What are the indisputable facts that this is true? Have they told you directly that they don't want to be with you tonight or that they never want to see you again?

3. "What are other possibilities?"

   Perhaps they tried to find you but couldn't. Could they be coming back? Could you have misunderstood what they said?

It is wise to remember that, as important as emotions are, feelings aren't facts.

—Barton Goldsmith, PhD

the self-esteem habit for teens

22. know it's okay if not everyone likes you

Alexis felt very upset whenever others didn't respond well to her. If they didn't compliment her or ask her to go out with them, or just didn't seem interested in getting to know her, she thought it was a personal rejection and told herself there was something wrong with her. Even though she had a solid group of good friends and most people enjoyed being with her, Alexis would worry about the few who didn't, and her self-esteem suffered. As long as she believed she wasn't good enough unless everyone liked her, she would never have healthy self-esteem.

Perceive It

When you think you're good enough only if everyone likes you, you're basing your self-worth on a false belief. As we've already established, every person has unconditional intrinsic value. And it's realistically impossible to be liked by *everyone*. Even if you try to be everything everyone else wants, there will be someone who doesn't like you for doing that! You yourself probably don't like all the people you meet, but that doesn't mean there's something wrong with them; it just means you don't click. It doesn't affect their value as human beings, and it doesn't affect yours if not everyone likes you.

Trying to get every single person to like you is an unachievable goal. It keeps you running on a never-ending treadmill that only exhausts you and denies your authentic self. As long as you strive for this, you'll never feel good about yourself. A wiser thinking habit is to understand that it's both okay and normal not to be liked by everyone. This thinking habit builds healthy self-esteem that, in turn, makes you a more likable person.

Believe It

It's impossible for anyone to be liked by everyone. I release that goal and focus instead on building healthy self-esteem habits.

Achieve It

On separate paper or in your journal, make lists of your favorite and least favorite colors, foods, clothes, and activities. A worksheet you can use for this is available at http://www.newharbinger.com/39195. Look over the lists and remind yourself that these things aren't inherently good or bad because of which list they're on. The items on your "least favorite" lists just don't suit you as well. The same goes for people. There are probably some people you don't like so much, but that doesn't make them bad or wrong; it just means they don't suit your personality as well. And there are other people who *do* like them. This is true for whether others like or dislike you, too.

Next, make a list of people you've been worried about getting to like you. Look at these names and remind yourself that their not liking you is not a reflection of your worth. Make a conscious decision to change this thinking habit, let these people go from your worries, and move on with your life. The next time you see them, smile and silently wish them well. Then focus on the friends you do have and create healthy self-esteem.

Really, Hagrid, if you are holding out for universal popularity, I'm afraid you will be in this cabin for a very long time.

—J. K. Rowling

23. refuse to have a pity party

Emily's friends were getting tired of her moaning and groaning. Every time something went wrong in her life, she complained about it over and over. She'd look dejected and say, "Listen to what happened to me now!" Then she'd talk about it for days. Finally, Jasmine approached her. "It's not that we don't care about you," she said. "We just get tired of your self-pity habit. It doesn't help anything, Emily; it just makes you and all of us tired. We're willing to listen and support you, but you have to start thinking more positively so you can actually help yourself and make things better."

Perceive It

People are said to be having a *pity party* when they wallow in their suffering or misfortune. They think about their current struggles over and over and say things like "Poor me" and "My life is awful and it'll never get better; I'm so unlucky." Pity parties are counterproductive to healthy self-esteem. They make you feel worse about yourself instead of better. They don't solve your problems; they just feed negativity and helplessness.

The difference between self-pity and compassion is that compassion is a positive thinking habit that helps you be gentle and kind with yourself and gives you more energy to make change. Self-pity is a negative, unproductive thinking habit that keeps you focused on your sorrows and decreases your energy for change. Refusing to have a pity party is a positive step toward healthy self-esteem.

Believe It

When something goes wrong, I treat myself with compassion but refuse to make things worse by having a pity party.

Achieve It

Sit quietly and comfortably and close your eyes. Take a few deep, peaceful breaths and relax. Think about the last time you gave yourself a pity party. Picture yourself sitting at the head of a big table. If you shared your self-pity with others, picture them at the table with you. Imagine that you see drooping gray streamers, popped balloons, melting ice cream, and a crumbling cake. Everyone is listening to a recording of you complaining over and over. See that your guests are bored and annoyed; they're tired of being there and can't wait for the party to be over so they can leave. There's a large banner on the wall reading "Poor me!" Feel the deep negativity that permeates the room. Then imagine yourself standing up and making the announcement: "This pity party is over!" Watch as you turn off the recording, throw the decorations and food in the garbage, and begin to smile. See both your own and your guests' faces light up. Instead of wallowing in self-pity, you start making a plan for how to make things better. Feel the new positive feeling throughout your mind and body. Set an intention to release the thinking habit of self-pity.

Self-pity is our worst enemy and if we yield to it we can never do anything good in the world.

—Helen Keller

24. accept your journey

Dylan felt uncomfortable as he listened to his younger brother talk about starting a business after high school. Zach had always been good at fixing cars and engines and knew he wanted to run his own automotive shop someday. Dylan had no idea what he wanted to do, and he was two years older than Zach. Dylan's uncle saw the look on his face. "Don't worry," he said. "You don't have to know right now. I went to nursing school and ended up owning a pet store—life has twists and turns! If you think you should know everything already, you'll just feel frustrated. Accept that life's a journey and take it one step at a time. You'll get where you need to go."

Perceive It

Teens especially can feel frustrated or discouraged when they don't have all the answers to their life path. You might think there's something wrong with you because you have no solid idea about your future or who you really are, and you may not even be sure which classes to take next term or which sweater to wear Friday night. If you think you should have all these answers but don't, you'll feel bad about yourself.

It's important to know that not knowing is both normal and okay. Whether you're a teen or older, seeking answers is an ongoing part of life. If you recognize life as a journey with new information and experiences around every bend, you understand there's always further to go and more to learn. Not knowing all your answers is a normal part of being alive. When you make it a habit to accept this idea, you'll have healthier self-esteem.

Believe It

It's okay if I don't know all the answers about myself; that's part of life's journey.

Achieve It

Help yourself feel more peaceful about the unknown with this breathing exercise. Sit quietly and comfortably, close your eyes or lower your gaze, and put your attention on your breath. Take a few gentle breaths, and notice where the air goes. It might enter your nose or mouth; it might move into your throat, lungs, or abdomen. Follow your breath's journey for a while with an attitude of curiosity and acceptance instead of judgment. Know that wherever your breath goes is okay. As you inhale, think or say, "Accept my journey" and as you exhale, think or say, "Release worry." Then as you breathe peacefully, picture yourself walking down a winding road. See yourself feeling calm and content even though you can't see around the bends ahead of you. Notice the sights and sounds around you as you approach your journey with acceptance and curiosity. Continue breathing peacefully and following this scene for as long as you'd like. Later, build the habit of remembering these accepting thoughts and images whenever you feel upset about the unknown.

Be patient towards all that is unsolved in your heart.

—Rainer Maria Rilke

25. find more than one source for self-esteem

Tony was skilled at video game design and came up with ideas everyone loved. He planned to study digital arts and build a career around his talent. When Tony got positive feedback on his projects, he felt good about himself. But when he made mistakes or didn't like his outcomes he felt worthless—because he based his self-esteem solely on his design skills. Gabriella excelled in hands-on work and loved helping her dad do home renovations. She usually got positive feedback about her skills, but not always. Because her self-esteem also came from skiing, volunteering with the homeless, and believing in her intrinsic value, Gabriella felt good about herself even if she had an off day at work with her dad.

Perceive It

The sources of your self-esteem are the things that help you feel good about yourself. They might be inner qualities like honesty and flexibility, talents and skills like photography or engineering, or healthy beliefs such as "I have intrinsic value" or "I'm equal to everyone else."

When you have more than one source for self-esteem, it's easier to keep it up.

For example, if you feel good because you can pitch a no-hitter and are also a valued employee, on a day your pitching is terrible you can still feel good about yourself because you worked well at your job. But if your only source of self-esteem is pitching, and you throw poorly for two weeks straight, your self-esteem will drop. People with healthy self-esteem make a habit of finding more than one reason to feel good about themselves.

Believe It

I recognize and remember that there are many reasons to feel good about myself.

Achieve It

In your journal or on separate paper, make a list of everything that builds your healthy self-esteem. Then write the percentage each contributes. For example, if you've written "good at gymnastics," "good at flute," "my parents' approval," and "I'm a nice person," and they all contribute equally, write "25%" next to each. If it's more or less, divide the percentages accordingly. (You might have "gymnastics—20%," "flute—10%," "parents' approval—20%," and "niceness—50%.") Next, draw a large circle and divide it into labeled sections—like pie slices—with your percentages determining the size of each slice. (In the above example, there would be four slices, with "niceness" written in the biggest, "flute" in the smallest, and "gymnastics" and "parents' approval" in the other two.) When you're done, observe your self-esteem pie. If you have only one or two slices, think of some more. (Everyone deserves to write "my intrinsic value," and because you're reading this book, you can write "desire to grow.") If you have a hard time, ask someone who knows you well for help. Try to keep at least three slices in your pie at all times. Then if you're feeling down in one area, remember you've got more than one reason to feel good about yourself.

The inward journey is about finding your own fullness.

—Deepak Chopra

positive actions

The activities in this section teach behavior choices that help create healthy self-esteem. This means you generally choose how to act based on integrity, responsibility, and confidence in your authentic self. You'll feel good about yourself when you make these choices, and when your positive actions create positive outcomes you'll feel even better. Of course, no one makes positive choices 100 percent of the time. If you choose a negative action, you can just notice it, accept it, and then do what's needed to fix it. You don't have to let an occasional poor choice send your self-esteem plummeting.

Although it's not essential to be using the positive thinking habits from part 1 before you start working on your actions, positive thinking can make it easier to choose positive behaviors. Keep this in mind as you move forward, as well as the facts that your self-esteem is in your hands, you have intrinsic value and worth, and your authentic self is your best self. Just as with thinking patterns, the more you practice these positive actions, the sooner they will become your new habits and build healthy self-esteem.

26. get to know your authentic self

When Kiara took a personality survey in sociology class, she was surprised to learn she was classified as both an adventurer and a mediator. She'd never thought of herself in these ways and realized she didn't know herself as well as she'd like. Her teacher suggested she keep a journal about her thoughts and feelings and try listening to herself more. After a few months, Kiara realized she'd been hiding a lot of her authentic self to be who she thought she "should" be, which often made her feel frustrated and unfulfilled. She realized she liked her authentic self more than her false self. As Kiara thought and acted from her true self, she started feeling happier, having more fun, and forming more sincere friendships.

Perceive It

Your authentic self is who you are before you try to be anyone else. A lot of us don't know our authentic selves well because we spend more time paying attention to others. We watch characters on TV and in movies, contemplate other people's lives on social media and in the news, and observe the friends and family members we see every day. We spend a lot of time looking outward, but not as much looking inward.

To truly feel good about yourself, you need to find out who you really are. Getting to know your authentic self is a show of self-respect and self-compassion. You deserve to discover and explore all the facets of your likes, dislikes, dreams, desires, beliefs, and character traits. Building the habit of paying attention to what's deep inside you strengthens your sense of self and reminds you of the gifts you bring to the world. This helps create healthy self-esteem.

Believe It

I make a habit of listening to my authentic self so I can know who I really am.

Achieve It

Listening to your intuition or "gut feeling" can connect you to your authentic self. This internal voice helps you choose a shirt, a friend, or an activity because you genuinely like them, not because they're cool by someone else's standards.

To get in touch with your intuition, sit quietly, close your eyes, and relax. Take a few peaceful breaths, and clear your mind. Imagine that at this moment you've stopped being anything that isn't true for you; you're being only your authentic self. Take a few moments to feel this as reality. Then slowly ask yourself the following questions and listen for the first answers that come. What is your deepest desire? What is your greatest goal? What are your strongest dreams? What are you passionate about? Let your intuition bring the answers from your authentic self. Then slowly open your eyes, and on separate paper or in your journal, record the first things that come to mind in response to these prompts: five things you like, five things you dislike, five things you believe strongly, five things you are passionate about, five things you would love to do, five things you would never do, five qualities you'd like to be known for, five things you'd like to contribute to the world. At http://www.newharbinger.com/39195, you can download a template for this purpose. Finally, using your answers as keys to your authentic self, write a description of who you really are.

When you know yourself you are empowered. When you accept yourself you are invincible.

—Tina Lifford

27. live from your authentic self

Josh didn't think his real self was "good enough," so
he tried to be whoever he thought others wanted him
to be. With his school friends he acted a little crazy.
Around girls he was a comedian. With his hockey
friends he acted tougher. Eventually, he felt exhausted
from always trying to be someone else. He decided
to stop pretending and just accept and live from his
authentic self—who he really was deep down inside.
As he did this, Josh felt more relaxed, happier, and
good about himself. His natural personality, strengths,
and talents flourished, and he knew people liked him,
not someone he was pretending to be.

Perceive It

You were born with a distinct combination of energy
and potential that makes you different from every other
human. Your life has a path all its own and makes a unique
contribution to the universe. Your greatest promise and
capacity lie in your authentic self because that's who
you're supposed to be, just like a dog is supposed to be a
dog, an eagle an eagle, and a rose a rose.

Although people you admire can be good role models, trying to be someone else only leads to failure—like a dog trying to be an eagle or a rose trying to be an orchid. Accepting and living from your authentic self, listening to your own heart, and honoring your own desires, dreams, and skills is the only way for you to truly thrive. When you respect, nurture, and act from who you really are, you create healthy self-esteem and can live your best life.

(Note: Your authentic self will lead to your highest good. If you think you're acting from your true self but are getting into trouble, talk to an adult you trust about how to rethink your choices.)

Believe It

I honor and live from my authentic self because that is my best self.

Achieve It

Based on your answers in activity 26, in your journal or on separate paper make a list of thoughts and actions that are true to your authentic self; for example, your authentic self might play the trombone, never drink tea, speak up for minority rights, dislike science fiction, wear denim every day, and laugh a lot. Over the next few days, pay attention to when you act from your authentic yourself and when you don't. Notice who you feel more or less comfortable being your authentic self with—your friends, family, teachers, or others? Next, choose a situation where you want to act more from your authentic self. Then sit quietly and comfortably and close your eyes. Take a few relaxing breaths, and picture yourself in that situation. Imagine you're completely comfortable being your authentic self, and picture an entire scene where you stay true to that goal. Use your five senses to create the details, and make the visualization as real as possible. Affirm that you feel safe and secure in this situation. Repeat this as often as you like and then set the intention to achieve this goal in real life. Notice how it feels and how people respond when you act from your authentic self.

Be yourself; an original is worth more than a copy.

—*Suzy Kassem*

28. use mindful breathing to stay calm and clear

When Ella felt anxious, she made things worse by focusing on negative thoughts. While waiting to give her oral presentation, she worried she'd mix up her words, forget her main points, or say "um" a lot. She told herself she was terrible at this. The more she worried, the more tense she felt: her jaw tightened, her heart raced, and her palms began to sweat. When she focused on her breath instead, her muscles relaxed and her mind cleared. She felt more centered and calm and could choose more soothing thoughts. She gave a better presentation and felt good about herself.

Perceive It

Mindful breathing simply means paying attention to your breath. When you inhale or exhale, you notice the air move in and out of your body through your nose or mouth. You feel the expansion of your lungs; the rise and fall of your chest, shoulders, or abdomen; and any other sensations that occur. Most people aren't used to doing this because our attention is focused on other places. We're often rushed or doing two things at once. This makes our breathing more rapid and shallow, lowering the oxygen intake to body and brain. Less oxygen makes us tense up and have a hard time thinking clearly enough to make positive decisions.

Focusing on your breath even briefly helps it slow down and deepen. This increases the oxygen to your body and brain, relaxes your muscles, and clears your mind. Then it's easier to choose positive thoughts and act in ways that build healthy self-esteem. You can work with your breath anywhere, anytime, and in any situation without much effort or anyone else being aware. The habit of mindful breathing is one of the most basic and powerful tools to help you stay calm and centered in positive thinking.

Believe It

I use my breath to calm my body and clear my mind. This helps me choose positive thoughts and actions that create healthy self-esteem.

Achieve It

To start your practice of mindful breathing, try the suggestions below or think up your own:

- Take a deep, mindful breath first thing each morning to bring your body and mind together calmly as they get ready to move into the day.

- Anytime you find yourself thinking or acting in a negative way, take one or two mindful breaths to stop the cycle and break that thinking or behavior pattern.

- Take a few mindful breaths at a regular time each day, such as every hour, every time you eat, or every time you answer the phone. This keeps you more calm and clear throughout the day.

- Daily, or a few times a week, spend five to ten minutes just sitting quietly and breathing mindfully, releasing tension and negativity.

- Make mindful breathing the last thing you do at night, clearing your mind of the day's activities and challenges, relaxing your body, and preparing you for a peaceful night's sleep.

If you know the art of breathing, you have the strength, wisdom, and courage of ten tigers.

—Chinese adage

29. manage your feelings

Ryan had a "short fuse," and it was causing him problems. The smallest irritation felt huge and was hard for him to handle. When he held his anger in, he got stomachaches and headaches; when he let it out, he exploded at people rudely. He knew he should respond differently and felt bad about himself because he couldn't. Ryan's doctor said he could learn new ways to act. Taking deep breaths would help him think clearly so he could choose healthier responses. Physical movement like stretching or sports would dissipate the stress chemicals that set him off. When Ryan managed his feelings better, his self-esteem improved.

Perceive It

Everyone has feelings, and we have a right to all of them. What we do with them, however, can be helpful or harmful. When you manage your feelings appropriately, you foster good health in your body, mind, spirit, relationships, and self-esteem. When you don't, your feelings can build up and cause physical, emotional, and social problems. A simple four-step plan can help you build the habit of managing your feelings well:

the self-esteem habit for teens

1. Name your feeling. (For example, you might feel disappointed, thrilled, nervous, irritated, content, or sad.)

2. Accept it. Remind yourself it's okay to feel anything that arises.

3. Express it in a way that doesn't hurt you or anyone else. (For example, sing, cry, write, swim, breathe deeply, draw, speak, dance, throw a football, play piano, or stretch.)

4. Do something to take care of yourself. (Listen to music, ask for a hug, call a friend, take a nap, or whatever helps at the moment.)

Believe It

I accept all my feelings and release them safely so I don't hurt myself or anyone else.

Achieve It

The next time you feel a strong emotion, try using the four-step plan described above. If you need ideas for safely releasing feelings, try one of the following techniques or brainstorm other safe ways that might work for you. When you build the habit of managing your feelings, you'll raise your personal and social confidence and your self-esteem.

Speak. State your feeling out loud, such as "I feel so, so sad right now," or "I feel so frustrated I could scream!" or "I'm feeling really disappointed," or "I am feeling such joy!"

Write. At the keyboard or on paper, write anything you want about how you're feeling. Forget about grammar, spelling, and punctuation, and just let whatever's inside you flow out. No one has to see what you're writing, and you can delete or shred it when you're done.

Draw. With crayons, markers, colored pencils, pencil, or pen, try putting your feeling on paper without using words. Let shape, color, line, or texture show what your feeling would look like if you could see it. Remember, this isn't art class; the goal is just to get your feeling outside of you.

Move. Stand up and move. Do whatever feels good—walk around the block, stretch your arms and legs, swim, pound pillows, go for a run, play tennis—or whatever is safe and possible in your situation. Moving physically releases the emotions so you can regain balance.

Breathe. Stop and take a few deep breaths. Imagine yourself inhaling peace and stability and exhaling your emotion.

Never let your emotions overpower your intelligence.

—Kenneth Jamal Lighty

30. learn to tolerate discomfort

Juan was stuttering and blinking his eyes a lot when he talked. His mom said it was a sign of anxiety, and because he couldn't stop by himself, she suggested he see a counselor. Juan felt really upset at that thought. He couldn't imagine telling a stranger his personal problems; that just made him feel more anxious. But when he finally got through the first meeting, Juan realized the counselor was nice and had the skills to help him. He decided it would be worth tolerating the initial discomfort to put an end to his anxiety. After he had been working with the counselor, his self-esteem rose, both from learning new skills and from doing something he originally felt nervous about.

Perceive It

If we run from everything uncomfortable, we'll be running for the rest of our lives. Many life experiences bring discomfort, and most goals worth achieving don't come without effort. Learning to tolerate discomfort helps you build inner strength, realize your courage, and achieve more of your dreams. There is always something to be gained from tolerating discomfort, whether it's reaching your goal or simply growing stronger emotionally.

You can tolerate discomfort more easily by working with your breath and your thoughts. Taking a few calming breaths brings oxygen to your brain and helps you choose positive thoughts, such as "This is only temporary, I can handle it," or "I know I can get through this," or "People tolerate worse things than this; I can do this." When you view discomfort as a temporary state that when endured will bring great rewards, you can transcend it and use it as a powerful tool. Strengthening your ability to handle discomfort also strengthens healthy self-esteem.

Believe It

I tolerate discomfort to gain the rewards that follow. This helps build my healthy self-esteem.

Achieve It

Reinforce the idea you can tolerate discomfort by trying this: Spend at least one hour today using only your non-dominant hand (when safely possible) for everything you do. If you are left-handed, use your right hand for your tasks; if you are right-handed, use your left hand. This could include brushing your teeth, getting dressed, combing your hair, eating meals, writing, playing games, typing, turning pages, opening doors, carrying books, petting your cat, opening mail, using your phone, and more. The longer you do this, the more deeply you ingrain the message into your brain that discomfort doesn't stop you from achieving your goals. Also, the longer you practice, the more you realize your own capacity. This fact gets stored in your memory, and the next time you're faced with an uncomfortable situation, you'll remember with confidence that you can make it through.

At the end of the day, on separate paper or in your journal, make a list of things you'd like to accomplish in the next week, month, and year. Next to each, describe any discomfort you might have to tolerate to reach this goal. Then take a few minutes to visualize yourself confidently moving through each uncomfortable situation and finally succeeding. The next time you face discomfort, remind yourself you're in the habit of tolerating it, not running from it. When you act from this belief, you'll build healthy self-esteem.

The world breaks everyone and afterwards many are strong at the broken places.

—Ernest Hemingway

the self-esteem habit for teens

31. set realistic goals

Jada wanted to sponsor a charity relay at school but it was almost time for summer break. She felt frustrated and annoyed when she couldn't pull it together in time. The principal suggested she start planning now for the next school year and break her goal into small steps. Jada formed a committee over the summer, set monthly short-term goals, and completed the work step by step, and the relay took place the following spring, raising over $10,000 for needy children. Jada felt good about herself and learned to continue the habit of setting realistic goals.

Perceive It

One of the main reasons people don't achieve their goals is that they set them too high. If you spend most of your time on the couch and set the goal to run a half marathon in two weeks, you're setting yourself up for failure. If you set a goal to start training this week and run a half marathon in six months, you've got a better chance of achieving it.

Goals that can be achieved more quickly are called *short-term goals*. Goals that take more time to accomplish are *long-term goals*. Most long-term goals are best achieved by setting short-term goals within them. For example, if your long-term goal is running the half marathon, your short-term goals could include buying good shoes, starting to run two miles a day, and increasing to five miles a day. When you get in the habit of setting realistic goals, you have a better chance of experiencing success and creating healthy self-esteem.

Believe It

I break bigger goals into smaller steps so I have a better chance of achieving them.

Achieve It

On separate paper or in your journal, make a list of your dreams and goals. Choose one and create a staircase of steps to lead you there. Draw a large vertical rectangle on a piece of paper to represent a staircase. Divide the shape with evenly spaced horizontal lines from bottom to top. These are your stairs. At the top of the staircase, write your long-term goal. It could be anything from "break my own free-throw record" or "pass geometry class" to "visit

Antarctica" or "teach Spanish." At the bottom of the staircase, write today's date. Then think about all the steps necessary to achieve your long-term goal. On the horizontal stair lines from the bottom up, write these steps in the order they'd need to be done, with one step on each line. (Add or subtract lines as necessary.) For example, if your long-term goal is to break your free-throw record, your steps leading up to that might include "ask the coach for pointers on how to improve," "lift weights twice a week," "visualize myself completing the shot every night before I go to sleep," "practice in the gym after school three times a week," "keep trying until I succeed." Once you've completed your list of steps, next to each one write an approximate date of when you could realistically achieve it. Reinforce your intention to complete these short-term goals by deciding what you can do today to work on your first step.

It's a cinch by the inch but it's hard by the yard.

—Familiar proverb

32. increase your peace

When things went her way, Gianna felt happy and liked herself; when they didn't, her mood swung low, and she'd put herself down. She spent a lot of time trying to control everything in her life so she could always feel good, but something new always happened to shake her up. "You're focusing your energy in the wrong place," her grandmother said. "We can't control everything outside of us, but we can control what happens inside." Her grandmother encouraged Gianna to spend a little time each day cultivating inner peace. "Do what feels calming for you," she said. "Things like peaceful music, stretching, quiet breathing, or repeating calming thoughts. When you practice this, it eventually becomes a habit that you carry along in life. You'll better handle whatever life brings and feel better about yourself when you're centered in peace."

Perceive It

Life will always bring challenges and things that don't go your way, but when you have a core center of peace, you're better able to face whatever arises. You have a steady place to respond from, so you can think clearly and make wise choices about your actions. When you bring that peace to every situation and person you encounter, there's a better chance you'll have positive experiences and relationships and build healthy self-esteem.

The good news is there is already peace within you; it just may be covered up with negative thoughts and feelings. It's said that when the artist Michelangelo was asked how he created the brilliant statue of David from a crude block of marble, he answered that David was already in the stone; he just chipped away the extra parts that covered him up. The habit of practicing calming activities will help you chip away at negative thoughts and feelings that cover your inner peace. Cultivating a calm inner core will make it easier to feel good about yourself.

Believe It

I nurture a center of calm within myself so my choices and actions originate from peace.

Achieve It

In your journal or on separate paper, make a list of activities that are calming or soothing to you. Choose from the items below or think of your own:

journaling	warm bath or shower
meditation	drawing
coloring	being in nature
taking a walk	petting an animal
peaceful music	exercise
deep breathing	playing an instrument
yoga	reading for pleasure
repeating affirmations	

Make a commitment to do one of these activities today or tomorrow, choosing a realistic time frame so you're sure to follow through. As you do the activity, let yourself enjoy feeling peaceful and relaxed. Focus on feeling calm in both your body and your mind, and affirm that you're releasing negativity and finding your inner core of peace. You can do this activity at the time you're feeling stressed, or on a regular basis even before stress arrives. Set realistic short- and long-term goals, such as starting with one time per week and gradually increasing to five. If the first activity doesn't work well, try another, or switch for variety. You can try a calming activity before making an important decision or facing a challenge. The more you practice the habit of increasing your peace, the more calm you'll become and the more you'll find success and healthy self-esteem.

You find peace not by rearranging the circumstances of your life, but by realizing who you are at the deepest level.

—Eckhart Tolle

33. use problem-solving skills

Lauren called her mom at work for the third time in a week. "I don't know what to do!" she said again. "You've got to learn to take care of some of these things by yourself," her mom said. "I can't talk now; I'm in a meeting." Lauren became easily overwhelmed when anything went wrong. She panicked and couldn't think clearly and immobilized herself. She felt so immature and got mad at herself for not being more competent. "Try this plan," her sister said. "We learned it in life skills class." Lauren read the acronym her sister gave her: STOP: Stop, Take a breath, Observe and be open to possibilities, Proceed. Lauren began following this simple plan and started feeling less helpless.

Perceive It

Challenges will always exist, and you'll always have to deal with them. No matter how old or smart or talented you get, you'll never have a problem-free life. However, you can learn how to handle problems so they don't overwhelm or debilitate you. When you can manage the challenges life brings and handle your problems in a pro-ductive way, you'll feel more confident about yourself.

the self-esteem habit for teens

Problem solving isn't a hit-or-miss operation. You can learn to approach problems knowing that you have the ability to tackle them. Whether you're facing a hard homework assignment, a relationship breakup, a difficult emotion, or a family conflict, you can learn effective tools to help you think things through and decide what to do. Getting into the habit of using problem-solving skills builds your confidence for handling life, increases your successes, and creates healthy self-esteem.

Believe It

I have a problem-solving plan that helps me handle any challenge. I make it a habit to use these skills so I don't feel helpless.

Achieve It

The STOP plan for mindfulness, described in *The Now Effect* by Elisha Goldstein and adapted here for problem solving, can help you stop feeling helpless and overwhelmed and begin to feel more confident about managing challenges. Try using this acronym the next time you're confronted with any difficult situation, from a lost set of keys to a hefty science fair project to an angry supervisor at your job.

S: Stop and take a break from what you're doing. Put down whatever is in your hands; stop all movement; clear your mind.

T: Take a breath. A few conscious breaths will calm your body and bring oxygen to your brain so you can think clearly.

O: Observe and be open to all possibilities. Without judgment, observe what's going on outside you and inside you and define it clearly. Then brainstorm endless ideas on how to take care of the situation. As in the exercise in activity 13: See Infinite Possibilities, come up with as many possible solutions as you can.

P: Proceed. Choose one of your solutions and try it. If it doesn't work well, try another. Keep going until you find the right answer.

Obstacles don't have to stop you. When you run into a wall, don't turn around and give up. Figure out how to climb it, go through it, or work around it.

—Michael Jordan

the self-esteem habit for teens

34. make positive decisions

Angelina didn't have enough money to buy both the bracelets she wanted. She went back and forth about which one to get, then realized she could have both if she just paid for one and slipped the other into her purse. But as she imagined the outcome, she realized her happiness of getting both would be overshadowed by her fear of being seen, her guilt over stealing, and the ramifications of getting caught. She put one bracelet back and paid for the other, walking out of the store feeling peaceful and good about herself.

Perceive It

Positive decisions are those that generate positive outcomes; negative decisions generate negative outcomes. Positive decisions can seem harder at first, but their benefits outweigh the discomfort. If you write an English paper yourself (positive decision), you'll have some discomfort in doing the work, but you'll increase your writing skills and feel good about your accomplishment (positive outcome). If you copy an English paper (negative decision), you'll experience guilt and bad feelings about cheating and possibly a failing grade and suspension or expulsion from school (negative outcome).

When you choose a positive attitude and remember the benefits of tolerating discomfort, you're better able to make positive decisions instead of negative ones. The more you make this a habit, the more your successes will increase and your healthy self-esteem will grow.

Believe It

I make positive decisions in order to get positive outcomes.

Achieve It

When you practice positive decision making with smaller-scale items, it will be easier to repeat when you face bigger challenges. Notice any decisions you make today, and count how many are positive. You could start with getting out of bed instead of sleeping all day, getting dressed instead of going out in your pajamas, or eating meals instead of going hungry. These might sound obvious, but they all count toward developing a habit.

Try to increase your number of positive decisions each day for the rest of the week. You could help with the dishes instead of complaining, start studying an hour earlier instead of waiting until you're tired, or clean

the self-esteem habit for teens

out your locker instead of stuffing more in. At the end of each day, in your journal or on separate paper, list the positive outcomes you gained from making these choices, and describe what would have happened if you hadn't. The next time you're faced with a decision with bigger consequences, such as whether to deceive someone, take the easy way out, or do something that would get you in trouble, your brain will see the consequences more quickly and urge you to make the positive choice. This habit of making positive decisions and gaining their positive outcomes builds healthy self-esteem.

Making good decisions is a crucial skill at every level.

—*Peter Drucker*

35. act with conviction

Taye and his friends were on a camping trip and hit
bad weather. It was cold and rainy, and they still had
another two miles to hike before they reached camp.
They were exhausted and hungry and had to portage
their canoes the rest of the way. Taye thought about his
choices: he could give up and sit in the rain all night
or he could keep going and make it to the dry tent. He
lifted the canoe over his head with conviction and told
himself over and over, "I can do this, I can do this."

Perceive It

Conviction is a strong belief and certitude. When you truly
believe in your intrinsic value and worth and your ability
to achieve your goals, you're able to face any challenge
with conviction. When the going gets tough, you keep
going, drawing on your inner strength and making positive choices. You know you can tolerate discomfort and
reap the rewards of seeing the challenge through.

If you think you're not able to act with conviction,
think again. If you're reading these words, you've already
done it. When you first learned to read, you had no idea
how to make sense of letters and their sound combina-
tions. But you persevered and kept trying—you acted with

the self-esteem habit for teens

conviction. You did the same thing when you learned to walk and talk, and faced a multitude of other challenges you've already met. If you make that kind of conviction a daily habit, you'll find success and healthy self-esteem.

Believe It

I refuse to be discouraged; I refuse to give up!

Achieve It

Acting with conviction is easier when you have an internal coach. Your coach is there to encourage you, create enthusiasm, and be a positive force of support. Coaches don't leave when the going gets tough, and they don't endorse giving up. Sometimes the only difference between those who achieve their goals and those who don't is the voice of that coach. When you're about to quit and someone says, "Hang in there, you can do it!" that may be all you need to keep moving ahead.

You can establish your own internal coach by creating personal messages of encouragement and inspiration. Think about what you'd want to hear when you're considering quitting. Record those messages in your journal or on separate paper and read them over regularly. Your coaching messages might sound like those below, or they could be very different. As long as they're positive, use whichever words work for you.

"Yes, you can do this!"

"Refuse to give up!"

"Refuse to be discouraged!"

"I know you can do this."

"Your conviction will see you through."

"You are not a quitter."

"You have the ability to see this through."

"You are strong enough to achieve this."

"Obstacles can't stop you."

When you build the habit of using these messages and acting with conviction, you'll foster healthy self-esteem.

I hated every minute of training, but I said, "Don't quit. Suffer now and live the rest of your life as a champion."

—*Muhammad Ali*

the self-esteem habit for teens

36. take responsibility instead of blaming

Saisha missed making the dance team by three points. The judges said her kicks weren't high enough. She practiced more, focusing on kicks, and tried out again the next season. This time she made the team and felt proud of herself for her improvements, and her self-esteem rose. Katherine missed making the dance team by three points. The judges said her kicks weren't high enough. Katherine said the judges were biased and voted only certain people onto the team. She didn't try out again because she said she didn't want to belong to a team of people who lied. She lost the chance to succeed, and her false judgment of the other girls made her feel bitter and bad about herself deep inside.

Perceive It

When we've made a mistake or things are really hard, it can seem easier to blame someone or something else. Maybe we don't want to admit we could do something wrong, we don't want to get in trouble, or we don't want to feel bad about ourselves or have others see us in a negative light. We try to avoid all this by laying fault somewhere else, but blaming never works because deep inside we know the truth.

When you take responsibility for your life, you have a chance to fix mistakes, make amends, and move on. When you blame, you lose that chance. You also lose the opportunity to feel good about your successes because taking responsibility means you can also own your achievements. The habit of blaming makes you a victim by giving the power for your actions and your happiness to someone or something else. The habit of taking responsibility gives you control of your life and your happiness and builds healthy self-esteem.

Believe It

I take responsibility for my own choices and actions. I admit my mistakes and enjoy my successes.

Achieve It

In your journal or on separate paper, over the next few days keep track of your actions, from taking a shower to finishing your art project. When you take responsibility for an action, record it under the heading "I Kept My Power"; when you blame someone or something else, record it under "I Gave Away My Power." When you give away your power, also record whom you give it to. For example, if you forgot to empty the dishwasher and admitted forgetting, you took responsibility and kept your power. If you blamed your sister for bothering you and "making" you forget, you gave away your power to your sister. Notice how often you keep or give away your power.

Build the habit of taking responsibility by using visualization. Sit quietly and close your eyes. Take a few relaxing breaths and clear your mind. Then picture yourself in a situation where you'd like to take responsibility instead of blaming. Imagine what you would say and do to own your actions. Imagine how others would respond and how you'd feel. If you notice discomfort, remind yourself to tolerate it long enough to reap the rewards. Picture the long-term outcome of taking responsibility for your actions and the feeling of empowerment you'd achieve for owning your own life.

Stop pointing fingers and placing blame on others.
Your life can only change to the degree that you accept
responsibility for it.

—Dr. Steve Maraboli

37. work with your weaknesses

Ethan felt so frustrated he could punch a wall. He'd tried seven times to get into a handstand on the rings but couldn't. He felt like an idiot and told himself everyone was laughing at him. Coach Walker tried making suggestions, but Ethan didn't want to hear them. He stormed from the gym, got his gear, and slammed three lockers on the way out. As he left the school, he heard the coach behind him: "Hey, Ethan, you'll never get into the handstand this way." "Yeah, I'll never get into it at all," Ethan said. "Don't worry, I'm quitting the team; I stink at gymnastics." "Stop and listen," the coach said. "Everyone has weaknesses, but quitting won't fix them. If you let me help, I can show you how to make it work. With a better attitude and a little practice, you could master a handstand and even more."

Perceive It

No one likes having weaknesses, but they don't have to damage your self-esteem. Because perfection doesn't exist on this planet, if you get down on yourself for not being good at everything or friends with everyone or smart in every subject, you're fighting a losing battle. A healthier habit is to accept your weaknesses and then, if necessary, work on improving them.

Some weaknesses don't matter much, like if you're not good at trigonometry and you want to be a massage therapist. Others matter more. If you have social anxiety and want to run for public office, you'll need to conquer that. But feeling bad about yourself for having weak or vulnerable areas doesn't help improve them and only lowers your self-esteem. When you can look at your shortcomings objectively, you have a better chance of both accepting them and working with them in a positive way.

Believe It

I accept all parts of myself and make an effort to improve the areas that need work.

Achieve It

If possible, complete activity 7 on celebrating your strengths before starting this one. Then, on separate paper or in your journal, identify up to five areas where you need improvement. Maybe you have a hard time telling the truth, being on time, taking tests, winning at a particular game, or making friends. Think about each area and decide whether it's important in the big picture of your life goals. If you can't crack an egg without it shooting all over the floor and you want to be a pastry chef, you'll need to improve. But if you want to be an accountant and don't like eggs anyway, it doesn't matter. Then by yourself, or with someone you trust, list the areas you want to work on in order of importance, and set short- and long-term goals for each that will help you improve. Set a realistic timetable for taking the first step. As you go through this process, remember that the habit of working on weaknesses with a positive outlook will help you build healthy self-esteem.

Never be afraid to expose a weakness in yourself.
Exposing a weakness is the beginning of strength.

—*Robert Anthony*

38. face challenges head-on

Olivia's parents were in the middle of a divorce, and she heard them arguing on the phone every night. When she imagined her family breaking up, she felt so bad she thought she couldn't stand it. To keep from thinking about it, Olivia started drinking alcohol in her room before she went to bed. At first she thought it helped, but then she started sleeping through her alarm and missing classes, and her friends said she looked terrible. She realized hiding from the facts was even worse than facing them.

Perceive It

Ignoring or avoiding challenges doesn't make them go away; in fact, it usually makes them worse. When you try to get around struggles by making negative decisions, you just add more problems to the first. The poet Robert Frost once said, "The best way out is always through," and he was right. While it might seem harder at first, facing a challenge head-on is the only way to fully resolve it and be able to move ahead.

If facing a challenge brings up anxiety, you can take some calming breaths, try to manage your feelings, and then use skills like adjusting your attitude or identifying rewards for tolerating the discomfort. You can set short-term goals to help you move toward a solution, or ask for help if you need it. Because facing challenges is the only way to be able to change them, building this habit is the only way to find success. When you run from problems, you make yourself a victim; when you face them head-on, you have the chance to create healthy self-esteem.

Believe It

I face my challenges so I can solve them permanently instead of making them bigger.

Achieve It

Identify a current challenge you've been avoiding. This could be anything from working on a research paper to admitting that a relationship isn't working. Then, using your journal or separate paper when necessary, take one or more of the following steps to break your habit of avoiding and start a new habit of facing things head-on:

- List your *avoidance techniques*. These are actions that keep you from thinking about or doing something about your challenges, such as denying, procrastinating, using alcohol or drugs, overeating or undereating, self-harm, sleeping too much, lying to yourself or others, keeping too busy, having too much screen time, overfocusing on other people's lives, or anything that you know deep down keeps you from facing your difficulties.

- Admit it to yourself. Say out loud or write down—without judgment—what you're doing to avoid your challenge.

- Tell someone else. Admitting your situation to a trusted friend, family member, or adult in your life helps release the energy of the avoidance habit. You free yourself to think about this openly and may also get support from the person you confide in.

- Spend five to ten minutes or more relaxing and visualizing yourself taking the steps to face your challenge. Visualize your ability to tolerate discomfort and the relief and pride you feel when you address the problem head-on.

- Take one step. Even if it's a small one, take it. Every step behind you is one less that's still ahead. Eventually, you'll reach your goal and reap the rewards of a job well done. Set the intention to continue facing your challenge, one step at a time.

Running away from a problem only increases the distance from the solution.

—Author unknown

39. turn things around

Andrew was caught vandalizing lockers and spray-painting graffiti on the field-house walls again. He felt like a loser, so he figured he'd act like one. "Getting in trouble is the one thing I do well," he thought. To his surprise, Dean Meyer didn't suspend him. "I'm sending you to Children's Hospital," he said. "You'll pay back your damage by doing art projects with terminally ill kids." At first Andrew thought it was a trick, but the dean said he was a good artist and just needed to turn his life around. Andrew didn't think that was possible; he'd always been a troublemaker—that was all he knew. But after a couple of weeks watching sick kids' faces light up as he painted and drew with them, Andrew felt something shift inside. He felt good about himself for the first time and thought maybe he could bring something positive to the world.

Perceive It

Sometimes we do things we regret, or our actions get us into trouble. Sometimes we make mistakes that seem too big to be fixed or let go of. We all experience this at some time in our lives. And when this happens, it's not unusual to have doubts about yourself. You might wonder if this mistake was too big to correct, if it will change your life forever, or if you've gone too far to turn back.

At these times, it's important to remember that it's never too late. You may have made a negative choice and experienced a really negative outcome, but in the very next moment, you're given the chance to start fresh and try again. Your mistake might seem insurmountable, but your innate value has not changed. You can make the decision to move up from where you are instead of continuing to spiral down. No matter what has happened, you can always choose differently at the next moment; you can turn things around. When you practice this habit, you move past big mistakes and create healthy self-esteem.

Believe It

No matter what I've done wrong, I can always make the choice to turn it around and get back on track.

Achieve It

At the top of a piece of paper or in your journal, write something you've done wrong. Then turn the page upside down, and write a solution to how you can turn things around and make them better. Choose from the following ideas or think of your own: apologize, make amends, create positive thoughts, forgive, admit your part in the problem, pay the consequences and move on, clean up what you messed up, ask for help, try a new way of behaving, do something nice for someone, give love, believe in yourself. If you get stuck or can't figure it out, ask an adult you trust to help you. Record the steps you'll need to take to get from your mistake to your solution. Affirm to yourself that you can turn this situation around if you first turn your thinking around, and then start taking one step at a time. Set some realistic short-term goals for working toward your long-term goal. Take the first step this week. Remember that any discomfort this challenge creates will be far outweighed by how good you will feel about yourself when you accomplish your goal.

No matter how far you've gone down the wrong road, you can always turn around.

—Author unknown

40. practice basic social skills

Anna was smart and fun, but social situations made her so uncomfortable she'd freeze up. "I never know what to say or how to act," she told her counselor. "Let's start with basics," said Ms. Bennet. "How would you like people to treat you?" "Well," Anna said, "be nice. Don't judge me, focus on my good points, listen to my thoughts, stuff like that." "So you do know how to be a friend," Ms. Bennet said. "Those are the same things everyone wants. You don't have to be the life of the party or a brilliant conversationalist; just start with the basics like being polite and kind. Act like the person you'd like to be with yourself."

Perceive It

Sometimes we think we need a special quality or an amazing personality to feel comfortable talking to people. We might think people who make friends easily have some magical trait that draws others to them. These thoughts create anxiety in social situations, especially with new people. We tell ourselves we'll have nothing to say or whatever we say will sound dumb. We forget our intrinsic value and equality to everyone else. We forget that other people have weaknesses and challenges, too, even if we can't see them.

Once you correct false beliefs and build positive thinking habits, the next step is to practice basic social skills. You probably know or use some already and just don't realize it. Talking to other people is a skill that can be learned and, like everything else, the more you practice, the better you get. Getting in the habit of using basic social skills like those suggested below can increase your confidence and build healthy self-esteem.

Believe It

Using basic social skills helps me start talking to people with confidence.

Achieve It

Memorize these six basic skills and ease them into your social interactions.

- Use good manners. What your parents taught you when you were growing up are still good rules to follow! Say "please," "thank you," and "excuse me," and don't interrupt when someone else is talking.

- Listen more than you talk. People quickly tire of those who talk only about themselves. Listening carefully is one of the best gifts you can give another person.

- Use conversation starters. If you can't think of anything to say, start with one of the five Ws: who, what, when, where, and why. (Who do you have for math this year? What are you doing over vacation? When does the new movie come out? Where did you get your backpack? Why did he give so much homework today?)

- Smile and be positive. Positivity makes us feel good. When you smile and talk and act positively, people enjoy being with you more.

- Give and accept compliments. Look for something you like and let the person know: "I like your sandals," "You're so thoughtful." When you receive a compliment, smile and say thanks. Downplaying a compliment is like refusing a gift.

- Remember the Golden Rule: treat other people the way you want to be treated. How would you like others to treat you? With courtesy, respect, compassion, acceptance, kindness? Practice those same qualities with others. That's what they want, too.

Politeness and consideration for others is like investing pennies and getting dollars back.

—Thomas Sowell

41. act assertively

Sarah thought her essay had been graded unfairly. She reacted passively by slumping in her chair and thinking how bad she felt. Her grade remained the same. Rachel thought her essay had been graded unfairly. She reacted aggressively by slamming her fist into her desk and swearing loudly. She got sent to the dean, and her grade remained the same. Sydney thought her essay had been graded unfairly. She reacted assertively by making an appointment with the teacher to explain her reasoning. The teacher listened, agreed, and raised her grade by five points.

Perceive It

There are three main communication styles: passive, aggressive, and assertive. If you think mean thoughts about someone who cuts in front of you in line, but say nothing, you're acting passively. If you shove that person, you're acting aggressively. If you calmly say, "Hi, I was already here. Is there some reason you're taking my place?" you're acting assertively.

Assertiveness is the most positive form of communication because its goal is to respect both your rights and the rights of others. When you develop the habit of acting assertively, you feel good because you're standing up for yourself, you're cooperating with other people, and you're doing it in a healthy way. You also get more positive outcomes in relationships. This all builds healthy self-esteem.

Believe It

Acting assertively helps me take care of myself and creates positive relationships with others.

Achieve It

Think of a situation in your life where you'd like to act assertively. Then pretend you're already an expert at being assertive, and imagine what you would say and do. In your journal or on separate paper, describe the scene as you picture it. Read over your ideas, and then take a few minutes to rehearse through visualization. First, sit quietly and comfortably, relax, and close your eyes. Then take a few calming breaths, and put your mind on your goal. Picture yourself in the situation you've identified. In your body and mind, really feel what it would feel like to have the security and serenity to act assertively. Imagine you can feel this through every cell of your body.

Then walk through the scene step by step in your mind. See the confident look on your face, listen to the clear way you express yourself, notice the respectful attitude you carry for yourself and others. Watch how you continue to breathe calmly, choose cooperative words, and stay balanced and centered throughout the whole scene. Whatever outcome occurs, imagine yourself remaining peaceful and at ease. When you're done, set an intention to try this in real life sometime in the next week.

The most important trip you take in life is meeting people halfway.

—Henry Boye

the self-esteem habit for teens

42. set healthy boundaries

*When Maria's friend Ashley continued to talk behind
her back and share her personal information even
though she'd asked her not to, Maria felt angry and
hurt. She didn't want to lose Ashley's friendship but
she didn't like being betrayed. She stopped spending
time with Ashley because she knew she could find a
friend who would be loyal and respect her. Kayla felt
cool dating Daniel because he was popular and smart.
But she didn't like him pushing her to be more intimate
than she wanted to be or being rude and harsh if she
didn't comply. Kayla felt conflicted but she broke up
with Daniel because she refused to be disrespected. She
knew she'd feel worse about herself if she stayed.*

Perceive It

Sometimes we want to be in relationships so badly we
forget to respect ourselves. We think being connected to
a particular person raises our value. But thinking you're
worth more because you're connected to someone else is
the opposite of healthy self-esteem. And if any relationship is abusive—where someone is bullying or in any way
disrespecting you emotionally or physically—it's time to

move on. Not only for your self-esteem but for your health and safety as well.

Setting healthy boundaries means putting limits on any kind of abusive behavior: physical, emotional, verbal, sexual, financial, digital, or stalking. Healthy boundaries could include speaking up for yourself, saying no to behaviors you're not comfortable with, asking for a change in behaviors, distancing yourself from someone who takes advantage of you, or leaving a relationship that's threatening or harmful to you. Setting appropriate boundaries to respect and protect yourself is healthy self-care and builds healthy self-esteem.

Believe It

I set healthy boundaries with others and don't continue relationships where I'm abused or disrespected.

Achieve It

Write your name in the middle of a separate piece of paper or in your journal, and draw a circle around it, allowing two or three inches between your name and the circle. Imagine this circle is your protective healthy boundary. Inside the circle, write the names of people in your life who treat you with respect. Outside the circle, write the names of anyone who doesn't treat you with respect or with whom you need to set a limit. Describe how each of those outside the circle treats you inappropriately and why you need to set the limit. Then identify ways you can do that; for example, you can say you won't tolerate the behavior anymore, ask this person to change the behavior, stop spending time together, or tell someone else about how this person is treating you. Make a commitment to yourself to take action on setting this limit in the next week. If you don't think you can do this by yourself, ask someone you trust for help.

Setting clear, healthy boundaries and enforcing them is empowering.

—Brian Luke Seaward

43. choose friends who value and respect you

Alondra felt confused. She'd always admired a certain group of girls at school and wished she were friends with them. Last week they asked her to a party and to go shopping. Initially Alondra felt excited, but while she was with them she didn't feel as good. Two girls suggested ways she could change if she wanted to hang out with them more. They gave advice about her hair, clothes, and the activities she should join. Their suggestions weren't really what Alondra wanted to do and made her wonder what was wrong with the way she was now. She started questioning whether being in this friend group would be as great as she'd thought.

Perceive It

The people you spend your time with can strongly influence who you are and how you grow. Those who like and respect your authentic self, who encourage you to follow your dreams, and have compassion for your feelings and needs are the ones who help you build healthy self-esteem. Those who like you only if you're acting the

156   the self-esteem habit for teens

way they want you to, who put down or make fun of your authentic self, or bully or manipulate you do the opposite.

You might choose friends because of their social status or because you feel pressured to hang out with certain people. You might be in a friend group where you're not comfortable being your true self. These connections don't build healthy self-esteem. The best friends you can have are those who respect themselves as well as others and understand that everyone has intrinsic value and worth. You can't choose everyone in your life, but you can choose many. When your friends treat you with respect and kindness, you're better able to do the same for yourself.

Believe It

I choose friends who sincerely accept and respect my authentic self.

Achieve It

In your journal or on separate paper, list the people in your closest friend group; or visit http://www.newharbinger.com/39195 to download a worksheet you can use. After each name, rate the following on a scale from 1 (low) to 5 (high): (a) how comfortable I feel being my authentic self with this person, (b) how much this person respects my authentic self, and (c) how much being with this person contributes to my positive growth. Then add comments to explain your ratings. For example, if you rate Caleb at 2 for (a), you might add: "I don't feel I can be my true self around Caleb. I feel nervous and always think I'm going to say something stupid."

When you're done, read over your ratings and comments. How does each of your friends affect your self-esteem? If any don't help you feel good about yourself, think about what you might change. Switching friend groups or letting people go out of your life can feel uncomfortable, so set small, realistic goals. You might start by changing the way you respond. Instead of letting Caleb intimidate you, try taking a deep breath and risk speaking from your true self. Choose one of these goals to try in the next week.

Celebrate the people in your life who are there because they love you for no other reason than because you are you.

—Mandy Hale

44. run your own life

Ben was shocked when his dad gave him the keys to his new sports car because he never let anyone else drive it. "I trust you," his dad said. "Just be back in an hour." Ben felt incredible driving this car. He picked up his friend Jack. "This is awesome!" Jack said. "Let's get Jose and Kevin." Ben hesitated, but there was still time, so he picked them up, too. "Take it out to Highway 7 and see how fast it'll go!" said Jose. "No," Ben said. "I can't." "Come on!" Kevin urged. "There's no traffic way out there. What can it hurt?" "I just know my dad wouldn't like it," said Ben. His friends taunted him until he finally gave in. On Highway 7 there were no other cars, so Ben stepped hard on the gas pedal, but he hadn't realized how fast the car would take off. When he hit the accelerator, the car fishtailed and spun into a ditch. The boys weren't hurt but they were stunned, and Ben's heart sank. He knew he was in trouble. He shouldn't have let them talk him into this.

Perceive It

When your friends try to get you to do something you don't want to do, it's called *peer pressure*. It can be hard to say no when other people are saying yes, but when you do something you don't want to do, you're not building healthy self-esteem; you're tearing it down. Making decisions about how to act based on the hope people will like you or just to go along with the crowd enforces the idea that you're not good enough just being your authentic self. This is a false belief.

Making your own decisions is the choice that creates healthy self-esteem. Not giving in to peer pressure doesn't mean you abandon all your friends, but it does mean you build inner strength. Going your own way doesn't mean you'll always be left out, but it does mean you'll feel peaceful inside. When you practice the habit of running your own life instead of letting others tell you what to do, you'll honor your authentic self, have more successes, and feel better about who you are.

Believe It

I feel good about myself by running my own life instead of letting others make my choices for me.

Achieve It

To make decisions that will build your self-esteem and help you run your own life, try asking, "Who do I want to be in the universe?" This question helps you focus on your values, dreams, and hopes for your life. It pulls your mind away from other people's opinions and puts it back on the power and potential of your authentic self. Instead of feeling pressure from the outside, you feel empowerment from the inside. The next time you're faced with peer pressure, instead of asking, "What does everyone else want to do?" or "What will they think of me?" ask, "Who do I want to be in the universe?" Think about the qualities you want to develop in yourself, the standards you want to live by, and what you want to contribute to the world. Then make the choice that's in line with that answer. It might not be the easiest choice at the moment, but if you tolerate that brief discomfort, the long-term gains will far outweigh the struggle.

I now know that every single bit of pain I have experienced in my life was a result of me worrying about what another person was going to think of me.

—Oprah Winfrey

45. surround yourself with positivity

Desiree's aunt gave her a recording of positive meditations. "For when you're feeling down on yourself," she said. "You know how you get in those ruts sometimes." A few weeks later, Desiree felt like she was in a negative cycle and couldn't get out. She listened to the meditations, and they did help. She still felt down but knew there was hope. The next day she listened again and copied some affirmations into her journal. Over the next week, she continued feeding herself positive thoughts and noticed her mood lifted faster than usual. Eventually, Desiree started listening to the meditations every night before bed and sticking her favorite positive messages in her locker. Her friends started noticing that Desiree was more fun to be around. When she made a habit of surrounding herself with positivity, it was easier to feel good about herself and her life.

Perceive It

It's a general principle of life that what is fed grows. Plants that get water, sun, and soil thrive. Animals and humans that get food, water, love, and attention flourish. Things that aren't fed wither and fade. The same is true for your thoughts and attitude: when you take action to feed your mind positive thoughts about yourself and your life, they become predominant and you grow a positive attitude.

Surrounding yourself with positive words, thoughts, quotations, pictures, and people is a way to grow positivity on a daily basis. Choosing to read books, listen to recordings, watch videos, or learn from people who are positive will help a positive attitude take root and grow within you. When you make it a habit to surround yourself with positivity, you'll build healthy self-esteem.

Believe It

I keep positive influences all around me to feed a positive attitude.

Achieve It

Look around your bedroom or other living space. Do the colors, objects, textures, and patterns give you a positive feeling? Do they make you feel happy and good about yourself? Do they reflect healthy self-esteem? Notice any words in your room—books, magazines, papers, posters.

What kind of messages do they send? Are you surrounded by uplifting, encouraging words? Ask yourself the same questions about your locker, electronic devices, car, or anything else in your environment that emits a positive or negative influence. Are you being fed positivity or negativity?

Start today to increase the positive in your surroundings. Pile uplifting reading material by your bed, affix positive quotations to your walls and screens, add positive music to your playlist, surround yourself with colors and designs you love, put up pictures of people who accept and respect your authentic self. Remove anything that sends you negativity. Get in the habit of reading, listening to, and looking at these positive influences, and you'll become filled with the attitude you need to build healthy self-esteem.

According to ancient wisdom, your environment reflects your life. Therefore, making improvements in one will positively influence the other.

—Neha Puntambekar

46. move your body

Noah joined the track team and ran and worked out regularly to improve his performance. When the season was over, however, he stopped the workouts and spent time in other activities. During the off-season, Noah noticed it was harder for him to stay upbeat and calm. He was more negative and nervous, and he'd feel more down on himself. His PE teacher suggested he start running again. "Exercise releases brain chemicals called endorphins," the teacher explained. "These help us feel good both emotionally and physically." When Noah began workouts again, he realized his teacher was right. In better physical condition he could think more clearly and manage his emotions, and it was easier to make positive decisions. His self-esteem went up again.

Perceive It

Exercise is good for keeping your body in shape, and it's a key factor in feeling good emotionally. Physical exertion sets off activity in your brain that increases the feeling of well-being. It also gets you breathing more deeply to bring extra oxygen to your brain, helping you think clearly. This combination makes it easier to choose positive thinking habits and feel better in every way.

You don't have to be a star athlete to get the benefits of exercise. Healthy movement can include walking, yoga, karate, lacrosse, hiking, tubing, snowboarding, weight lifting, soccer, tennis, bowling, golf, surfing, ballet, Frisbee, laser tag, cheerleading, basketball, and more. When you get in the habit of moving your body, it helps you create and maintain healthy self-esteem.

Believe It

I make exercise a habit so I can feel good both physically and emotionally.

Achieve It

Choose something physical you could do in the next few days. Think of a time that's realistic, and set the intention to follow through. Use these tips to help you:

- Pick something you like to do. Try to choose movement that brings you joy. If you think you should bike three miles every morning but don't like biking and aren't a morning person, chances are you'll quit before you even start. If you like what you do, you're more likely to keep doing it.

- Don't hesitate to think outside the box. You could take a dance class or you could dance in your bedroom with headphones. You could run on a track or you could run with your dog. You could play volleyball at the gym or in the sand at the beach.

- Keep it interesting. Try mixing things up a little—variety adds spice to life. If you used weight machines for two weeks, take a stretching class or go for a swim. If you always work out indoors, try going outside, or vice versa. If you usually exercise alone, try including a friend.

- Set realistic goals. Habits are easier to form if they're not too far out of your comfort zone. Feeling a little muscle ache means you've tried something new and might motivate you to try again, but not being able to walk means you pushed too hard and probably won't exercise again for a long time. Encourage yourself to keep going but respect your limits.

Try exercising in a consistent way for a few weeks and notice how it affects your self-esteem.

I've run my whole life—for more than exercise, for mental health.

—Wendelin Van Draanen

the self-esteem habit for teens

47. try new things

While Aarav was on vacation he went parasailing. He wasn't sure he wanted to, but his dad encouraged him so he went with his brother. As the rope was let out, the boys rose higher and higher. At first Aarav was having fun, but then he felt uncomfortable. They were climbing to one thousand feet, and even though he was strapped in Aarav didn't feel secure. The boat looked like a tiny speck below, and the rope looked like a thread. Aarav wasn't terrified, but he wasn't enjoying it either. He went up again the next day and still didn't like it. Aarav felt disappointed but also happy that he'd tried. "You did a great job of trying something new," his dad said. "That's an accomplishment in itself!"

Perceive It

Most of the time it's important to push through life tasks until you succeed. But succeeding isn't required for this habit; it's the trying itself that reinforces inner strength and builds healthy self-esteem. Trying something new helps you stretch beyond your current limits. You can feel good about yourself for acting with courage and moving into new territory. There is always the chance you won't succeed, but if the goal is simply to try, you achieve that just by taking the first step.

When you try something new, you benefit both from the attempt and from what you learn. For example, trying the high dive at the pool for the first time might end in a belly flop, but you can feel good about having the courage to give it a shot. You can also learn how to move or position yourself differently to make it work next time. Trying something new also broadens your horizons. You expand yourself a little each time you move in a new way, take in new information, or open your mind further. Even if you don't succeed, you can feel good about yourself for "succeeding at trying."

Believe It

I try new things to reinforce my confidence and courage.

Achieve It

On separate paper or in your journal, make a list of anything you've never done and would like to (safely) try. List both the smallest and the most monumental, such as move my bed under the window, eat a pomegranate, grow out my hair, bake bread from scratch, play badminton, go camping, write with purple ink, stand on my head, catch a firefly, ride the highest roller coaster, take a photography class, watch professional wrestling, learn Japanese, hike six miles, climb a mountain, or listen to new music. Your items don't have to be unusual, just new for you.

Next, divide the activities into two categories: "Every Day" for more common things and "Wow" for those really outside your norm. Choose one item from your "Every Day" list to do in the next forty-eight hours. Choose one item from your "Wow" list, and make a plan to try this in the next few months. When you complete a try, check it off your list. Keep adding to your list over time. The habit of trying new things keeps both you and your life interesting, contributes to learning and growth, and builds healthy self-esteem.

If you try anything...you have already achieved something wonderful, before you even begin.

—Sarah Dessen

48. wear a smile

Jacob sat on the exam table waiting for his annual physical. When Dr. Jennings walked in, his first question was "Are you feeling depressed today?" "A little," said Jacob. "How did you know?" "I can see it in your face and body," Dr. Jennings said. "Your mouth is drawn down, and your shoulders are sagging." "I've been feeling discouraged," Jacob said. "I have to take two classes over in summer school. I can't stop thinking how stupid I am." "Well, you'll never feel better with those thoughts," said Dr. Jennings. "Here's my prescription: start smiling." "What?" asked Jacob. "When you smile, you send a signal to your brain that you're feeling good," the doctor explained. "Your brain then releases chemicals that relax you and increase your good feeling, so you physically create happiness. That helps you stop the negativity and feel better about yourself."

Perceive It

Scientists who study smiling explain that using your facial muscles to raise your cheeks and lift the corners of your mouth sends a signal to your brain. Your brain then releases "feel-good" chemicals, such as endorphins and seratonin, that relax your body and increase your feeling of well-being. (Then you feel good, smile more, and the feedback loop continues.) When you're feeling good, it's easier to think positively, focus on the good in yourself, and create healthy self-esteem.

Studies also show that people who smile are perceived as more likable. When you practice the habit of smiling, others are more likely to want to approach you and get to know you. This, in turn, helps you feel good about yourself. It's important to note that you don't actually have to feel happy for the smile to work. Start up a smile even when you're sad or discouraged, and your brain will release the chemicals to help you get to happiness.

Believe It

I smile often to signal my brain that I'm happy about myself and my life.

Achieve It

To incorporate more smiling in your life, try the suggestions below or come up with your own.

- Every time you look in a mirror, put on a smile.

- Every time you look into someone else's face, put on a smile.

- Practice different smiles. Maybe you have a big grin, a subtle smile, a laughing smile, or others. See how many you can come up with.

- Watch other people smile, and smile back using the same type of smile they used.

- Connect smiling with mindful breathing: every time you stop to take a mindful breath, let that action send a smile to your face.

- When you notice negativity within you, shift your mood by immediately forming a smile, even if it's in opposition to what you're feeling.

- Add a smile to your morning routine of getting dressed. When you put on your clothes, put on your smile, too.

- Put a smile on your face when your head hits the pillow at night. Take a positive feeling into sleep with you.

A smile makes you master of yourself.

—Thich Nhat Hanh

49. look the part of healthy self-esteem

Nick's family moved a lot because his dad was in the army, and Nick often felt nervous starting at a new school. He wondered how people would respond to him, whether he'd make friends, and what the kids would be like. From making so many new starts, Nick learned he'd feel more confident if he looked and acted with confidence. So the first day he always wore his favorite jeans and a comfortable shirt that fit well. He worked out before school to release anxiety. He ate a good breakfast so his stomach wouldn't growl, and before he entered the building he'd affirm that he was a friendly person and he'd meet other friendly people that day. He made it a point to walk tall and smile. It took some concentration and energy, but this plan always worked for Nick. When he looked the part of healthy self-esteem, that's what he felt inside.

Perceive It

When you feel good about yourself, it shows physically. You stand or sit up taller, smile more, look less stressed, and move in a more confident way. Even when you're not completely confident, having the look of healthy self-esteem can help you feel it. This is partly because you're sending signals to your brain that you do feel good about yourself, and your brain perpetuates that feedback loop. Also, you're sending the social signal that you're happy, open, and want to connect, so your look is inviting to others and they're attracted to your cheerfulness and positivity.

Looking the part of healthy self-esteem can include being clean and well groomed, using good posture, smiling in a friendly way, having a happy and positive look on your face, looking into people's eyes when you talk to them, treating yourself and others with respect, and appearing comfortable being your authentic self. When you practice the habit of looking like a person with healthy self-esteem, you begin to create it.

Believe It

When I look and act confident and friendly, it helps me feel confident and friendly.

Achieve It

Choose one day this week to try an experiment. When you wake up in the morning, imagine you already have solid, healthy self-esteem. You feel confident in yourself and your relationships, you're happy to be alive, and you like your authentic self. Set the intention that all day, in every situation, with every person, you will act as if the healthy self-esteem you want is already yours. You'll show it in your eyes and your smile, in the way you walk and talk, and in the choices you make about your thoughts and actions. It doesn't matter how you felt yesterday or what's happened before. Today you'll have healthy self-esteem. Today you'll be the person you want to be. You'll feel the peace and happiness that comes from genuinely accepting and feeling good about yourself, both strengths and weaknesses combined. Try to keep this attitude as you go through the day, but remember it's okay if you slip up. If that happens, just notice it and get back on track. At the end of the day, think or write about how the experiment affected your self-esteem.

The best thing you can wear is confidence.

—Familiar proverb

50. ask for help

Brandon wanted to mow lawns in the summer to earn money. His first job was at the Lewins'. He'd never used their type of mower before and wasn't sure how to adjust the settings, but he didn't want to look dumb, so he just took a guess and began mowing. At first everything seemed fine, but when he mowed over an area with some tree roots, he heard an awful clunking noise, and the mower shut down. Brandon didn't know what was wrong and couldn't get it restarted, so he had to get Mr. Lewin. Mr. Lewin looked underneath and saw that the mower blade had been bent. "The deck wasn't set high enough," he said. "I wish you'd asked me before you started; this wouldn't have happened. Now I have to buy a new blade." Brandon felt terrible and paid for the blade himself.

Perceive It

Sometimes we think being capable and mature means handling everything on our own all the time. We don't ask for help because we'd feel humiliated and imagine people would look down on us. In reality, the opposite is true. While it's important to build problem-solving skills for manageable tasks, it's just as important to know when asking for help is the best solution.

The smartest and most successful people make a habit of asking for help when needed. The proverb "two heads are better than one" has stood the test of time because it's true: guidance from those with more experience or knowledge can bring you the right information to move ahead successfully. Learning something new from a teacher, mentor, or friend increases your own knowledge and your chances for success. This helps build healthy self-esteem.

Believe It

Asking for help when I need it is a sign of wisdom, not weakness.

Achieve It

Think of all the people who've helped you through your life to this point. These might be parents, other family members, teachers, coaches, friends, neighbors, doctors, counselors, or others. Someone held you up when you were learning to walk; someone steadied you as you learned to balance on a bike; someone explained numbers and counting as you learned to add. Because those people helped you, you were able to achieve your goals and feel good about yourself. No one looked down on you because you needed help with something new.

As a teen and young adult, you're learning even more. If you want to expand and grow and try new things, you'll find more success if you ask for help when necessary. On separate paper or in your journal, make a list of any challenges you're facing now where asking for help would be a wise choice. Then brainstorm a support list of anyone you know and trust who might help you with these projects, or any new people you might approach. Think about which person could best help with which challenge. Next to each name, write the person's phone number or email address and make a plan for when you'll contact that person. Keep this list for future use as you build the habit of asking for help.

I believe it is important we ask for help, not because we're weak, but because we want to remain strong.

—Les Brown

the self-esteem habit for teens

ending notes

You may have come to the end of this book, but if you really want healthy self-esteem, this won't be the end of your practice. The tools presented in these pages are meant to be used over and over, for days or weeks or months to come, until they become your new habits. Some of them may become easily ingrained, and others may take much longer to master. That's okay! We're all works in progress and can continue growing and improving for as long as we live. Remember to compare only to yourself and your own progress, and congratulate yourself for every positive step you take. Accept your journey, affirm your value and worth, and celebrate your authentic self—you're on your way!

acknowledgments

Heartfelt thank-yous to Tesilya Hanauer as always, for believing in my work and potential; Karen Schader again, for the great blend of fun and professionalism; Nicola Skidmore and Clancy Drake for their guidance and support; Cassie Kolias and Katie Parr for their patience and perseverance! And the whole staff at New Harbinger, who do their jobs well and make these books happen, bringing health and healing to so many people. I'd also like to thank Amy Blue, who once again burned up the research highway; my husband for continued cheerleading; and my whole family for understanding deadlines. And a special thanks to Susan Hoke and Larry Shapiro, who took a chance and started it all. It takes a village to write a book!

Lisa M. Schab, LCSW, is a licensed clinical social worker with a private counseling practice in the greater Chicago, IL, area. She has authored sixteen self-help books and workbooks for children, teens, and adults, including *The Anxiety Workbook for Teens* and *Beyond the Blues*. Schab teaches self-help workshops, conducts training seminars for professionals, and is a member of the National Association of Social Workers (NASW). You can find out more about her at www.lisamschabooks.com.

More ⏱Instant Help Books for Teens
An Imprint of New Harbinger Publications

**THE TEEN GIRL'S
SURVIVAL GUIDE**

Ten Tips for Making Friends,
Avoiding Drama & Coping
with Social Stress

ISBN 978-1626253063
US $17.95

**THE PERFECTIONISM
WORKBOOK FOR TEENS**

Activities to Help You
Reduce Anxiety &
Get Things Done

ISBN 978-162625-4541
US $16.95

**GET OUT OF YOUR
MIND & INTO YOUR
LIFE FOR TEENS**

A Guide to Living an
Extraordinary Life

ISBN 978-1608821938
US $15.95

**THINK CONFIDENT,
BE CONFIDENT
FOR TEENS**

A Cognitive Therapy Guide
to Overcoming Self-Doubt
& Creating Unshakable
Self-Esteem

ISBN 978-1608821136
US $16.95

**CONQUER NEGATIVE
THINKING FOR TEENS**

A Workbook to Break the
Nine Thought Habits That
Are Holding You Back

ISBN 978-1626258891
US $16.95

**THE GRIT GUIDE
FOR TEENS**

A Workbook to Help
You Build Perseverance,
Self-Control & a
Growth Mindset

ISBN 978-1626258563
US $16.95